BRITAIN SPEAKS OUT, 1937–87

A social history as seen through the Gallup data

Robert J. Wybrow

Director, Social Surveys (Gallup Poll) Ltd

MACMILLAN

First published 1989

Published by
THE MACMILLAN PRESS LTD
Houndmills, Basingstoke, Hampshire RG21 2XS
and London
Companies and representatives
throughout the world

Printed in the People's Republic of China

British Library Cataloguing in Publication Data
Wybrow, Robert J
Britain speaks out, 1937–87.
1. Great Britain. Politics. Attitudes & public
opinion, 1937–1987
I. Title
320.941
ISBN 0–333–39663–4 (hardcover)
ISBN 0–333–39664–2 (paperback)

Contents

List of Tables

Preface

Since its founding as the British Institute of Public Opinion in 1937, Gallup has been asking questions of the general public virtually every week, even through the dark days of the war. This book represents just a fraction of the thousands of questions which have been asked over the past fifty years or so, many at regular intervals. It attempts to show what the British public thought about events not only at home but in the wider world, and to chronicle their changing views on the issues of the day. Unless otherwise stated, the results contained herein are of adults in Great Britain and, for the statistically minded, are normally based on samples of around one thousand cases.

Due to the embarrassing wealth of data in the Gallup files - there have already been three single volumes published dealing with 1980, 1981 and 1985 - the author has had to be selective in his approach but hopes that the spread and depth of material used will satisfy most general readers.

For those interested in specific topics or particular periods, there are the files themselves, open for inspection at Gallup's offices. There are also two volumes (The Gallup International Public Opinion Polls : Great Britain, 1937-1975, Random House, 1976) which contain the bulk of the material for the first thirty-eight years and Gallup itself publishes a monthly report containing its public, political, social and economic data.

1 1937-1945 : The Formative Years

On 1 January 1937 Dr Henry Durant officially opened the doors of Gallup, under its first name, the British Institute of Public Opinion. In doing so he was holding up a new kind of mirror to our society which afforded insights so valuable that the process has gone on and expanded ever since, taken up by competitors, by academic institutes and by governments for the unique understanding it gives us of who we are, what we do and sometimes why.

British society in the late 1930s can be looked at via Gallup surveys under two quite different headings. What was life like for the British of two generations ago, what did they do and what did they think? Secondly, how did a people still not entirely recovered from the trauma of The Great War react to international tension and the prospects of another war itself? Times were hard. In June 1937 and in more detail a year later, it was reported that the average person thought that £4 a week was needed for a family of four to live decently. Even setting aside the many unemployed, the bulk of the labour force was earning distinctly less than this. In 1938 57 per cent of the public said that they were worse off than a year before. In fact the worst effects of the depression were beginning to disappear and the economy was beginning to move, but the British have had a gloomy view of 'next year' throughout a majority of the years in which Gallup has taken this particular sounding. However, there were diversions from a hard life not available to previous generations, in particular the cinema and the wireless or radio. In November 1938 Gallup reported that nearly half the adult population went to the cinema at least once a week, including 18 per cent who went at least twice a week. The theatre and in particular the music hall were losing out to the new medium and by March 1938 those who would prefer the theatre even if the seats were the same price were reduced to a minority of 40 per cent. Films in colour had recently been introduced and by January 1938 70 per cent of adults had seen one and the majority liked what they saw. The cinema of the time was largely escapist, and despite the intention of the BBC under Lord Reith to entertain, inform and instruct, it was diversion that people sought above all on the air.

In a survey in July 1937 people gave their favourite wireless programmes as variety (27 per cent), light or dance music (11 per cent) and plays and

1

classical music (6 per cent each). The BBC monopoly was being broken however by commercial stations in France and Luxembourg. By January 1938 68 per cent of people listened to such programmes, though only two thirds of them regularly, and strangely enough in the main they claimed not to prefer them to the BBC. One clue to this behaviour might have been that the BBC still set its face against dance music on Sundays: in December 1938 a majority of the public wanted the BBC to include a regular Sunday dance band programme. Football was high on the entertainment agenda and showed no signs of the financial and social problems it manifests today. The newly started football pools were proving popular - half the adult population participated, staking their sixpences, shillings or half crowns (May 1938). Certainly not all leisure, however, was spent before the cinema screen, the radio set or watching sport. Forty-four per cent of adults claimed in December 1937 that they kept fit in some way or another: out of these, 42 per cent mentioned games in general, 37 per cent hiking and 21 per cent physical jerks of some kind (jogging had not been heard of 50 years ago). With car ownership limited far more to the well-to-do than nowadays, the bicycle was a dominant form of independent transport, both for work and play. Considerations for safety led to a campaign for cycle tracks on main roads, and when asked in October 1937, the public was in favour of this by 75 per cent to 13 per cent against. Few have come about.

Despite the gathering clouds of war, people were looking for internationally agreed solutions then as now. In June 1937, 71 per cent of the public wanted Britain to continue to support the League of Nations. In practice it had been shown to be rather ineffective, particularly in the case of the Italian invasion of Abyssinia. Later that year in December, 72 per cent wanted Britain to remain a member of the League. Disarmament was an issue which did not go away until the outbreak of war itself. In the same survey, 49 per cent were in favour of an all-out reduction of armaments by international agreement, 24 per cent were against and the remainder were unable to express a positive opinion. Similar answers were given when the question referred specifically to the abolition by international agreement of military aircraft, the weapon of the time regarded as so fearfully destructive, as the bombing of Guernica in Spain had demonstrated.

So the British feared war and were looking for collective solutions, though by 1937 the ineffectiveness of the League of Nations had already been demonstrated and Europe was already less peaceful. In addition to Italy's defiance of the League, Franco had launched a right wing rebellion in Spain in 1936 which was, with the help of the Germans and Italians gaining valuable war experience, to end in victory in 1939. As late as

September 1938, 57 per cent of the British sympathised with the government forces in Spain, only 7 per cent with the fascist Franco regime and 36 per cent expressed no preference. Nevertheless there was a vocal minority in Britain who saw Franco as a shield against the evil of communism. The British were trying to comprehend fascism, not only in Spain but principally in Germany, and they were still trying to come to terms with the concept of communism. Thus in November 1937 when asked if they had to choose between fascism and communism, 26 per cent opted for fascism, 28 per cent for communism and 46 per cent couldn't say, indicating not a little confusion. That this mattered is evidenced by replies to a question in June of that year where 72 per cent of the public thought that Britain would inevitably be drawn into any future European war, and only 24 per cent did not. In the following month 36 per cent of men claimed they would volunteer in the event of such a war, 58 per cent refusing the idea, and only 19 per cent of women stated they would urge their husbands to join the colours.

1938

Turning to politics, it is remarkable to see how many issues of those times remain on the political agenda today. In March 1938 28 per cent of the public wanted to see Northern and Southern Ireland under one constitution, 26 per cent were against and a substantial proportion, 46 per cent, could not pronounce on this. Similarly, (April 1938) self-government for Scotland was mooted and 30 per cent were for, an equal number against, and a substantial 40 per cent unable to decide.

One survey evoked a legacy of the Great War. Due to the appalling casualties on the Western Front there were many women, now middle aged, who had never found a marriage partner, and in April 1938 82 per cent of the public were in favour of granting pensions of 10 shillings (50p) per week to spinsters at the age of 55. There were other pressures on women at a time of high unemployment. In contrast to our present ways of thinking, 56 per cent of adults thought that women in non-professional work should give up their jobs when they married, with 39 per cent against. In the case of trained women such as teachers and doctors, the proportions were 48 per cent for them giving up their jobs against 46 per cent thinking they should retain them.

These were some of the social and political issues of the time on which Gallup captured and recorded public opinion. The polls reported so far on particular issues and problems cast an interesting light on the conditions, attitudes and opinions of the British at that time. The principal value of such polls is not however to help historians of later generations but to inform the public of the time about the balance of opinion. To ensure that its results reached the public regularly and in a proper form, Gallup made arrangements to appear fortnightly in the weekly magazine, *Cavalcade*, during its first two years, and then switched to a national newspaper, The *News Chronicle*, in October 1938 on an exclusive basis. This arrangement persisted until the demise of that publication when Gallup switched to a contractual arrangement with The *Daily Telegraph*, always on the basis of controlling the form and content of what was stated. The arrangement has persisted for nearly all Gallup's research in the public domain until the present day.

Polls are equally famous nowadays for the light they throw on election campaigns as they are about individual political and social issues. Our sister company, American Gallup, had had a dramatic success in 1936 in forecasting the re-election of Franklin D. Roosevelt as President against a favoured Republican candidate, Landon. British Gallup had no such opportunity to demonstrate its powers, but started off by privately polling in four by-elections in 1938: West Fulham, Oxford, West Lewisham and East Norfolk. The Gallup studies indicated the correct winner in all four cases, with a small margin of error in each constituency. At West Fulham, won for Labour by Dr Edith Summerskill, the error was just 0.6 per cent, and was only marginally higher at 1.1 per cent in Oxford, where another illustrious parliamentarian, Quintin Hogg, won the seat. Flushed with this success, Gallup persuaded The *News Chronicle* to publish their estimate of the Batley and Morley by-election in March 1939. Gallup forecast a neck and neck race with a slight edge for the Conservative party, actually fighting under the Unionist label, but said the result was too close to call. In the event Labour held the seat with a slightly increased majority and the Gallup survey was shown to have under-estimated the Labour vote by 6.1 per cent. This was distinctly embarrassing for Gallup, but it redeemed itself later in May 1939. In the Hallam (Sheffield) by-election it correctly named the winner and was within 2.7 per cent of the winner's share of votes, normally regarded as an acceptable margin of error.

The first Gallup Poll to be published in The *News Chronicle* appeared on Wednesday, 19 October 1938. They had prepared the ground by explanatory articles on what an opinion poll was, at the time certainly a novel idea to the British public. By this time Hitler's Germany had taken over Austria with little resistance and now set its sights on the Republic of Czechoslovakia. Mr Neville Chamberlain had recently returned from Munich after having had discussions with Adolf Hitler, and stepped from his plane at Hendon aerodrome waving the agreement signed between the two parties, claiming that he had brought 'peace in our time'. This peace had been bought at the expense of partitioning Czechoslovakia. Following this, the Gallup survey showed that 51 per cent of the public were satisfied with Chamberlain as Prime Minister and 39 per cent were not. Support for him was largely from Conservatives though there was also a pacifist element supporting him among the opposition. Superficially this support was support for the appeasement policy with which he was so clearly identified. Nevertheless, the public did not, when asked other related questions, indicate that they had any confidence in the idea that peace had been assured. In the same survey 78 per cent thought that a National Register should be compiled immediately listing everyone available for civilian or military duty in wartime; 80 per cent favoured increased expenditure on armaments; and 93 per cent did not believe Hitler's claim that he had no more territorial ambitions for Germany in Europe. The British public was becoming aware of the nature of the Nazi regime, and of the inevitability of resistance to it rather than appeasement, even if this led to war. Thus, in November 1938, more news about the ill-treatment and indeed persecution of the Jews in Germany filtered through leading to a Gallup question on the subject. The Nazi Propaganda Minister, Goebbels, had claimed that the treatment of Jews in Germany was no concern of anyone but the Germans, and 73 per cent of the British public regarded this as an obstacle to a good understanding between Britain and Germany. Only 15 per cent said it was no obstacle, and 12 per cent could not decide on the point. At the same time Neville Chamberlain's standing was becoming weaker and there was discussion of a new political grouping under the heading of Mr Eden, then out of office. Gallup showed there would be support for it though it never came about. Later that year, again on the dominant theme of the German threat, 75 per cent of the public stated that Hitler should not get the German colonies back that had been lost as a consequence of her defeat in the First World War, and just over half (52 per cent) of the public were prepared to fight to prevent them falling into his hands.

1939

By 1939 a third country had joined the Gallup group - IFOP in France. (Almost fifty years later there would be more than forty countries in Gallup International, spread across all continents.) The opportunity was then taken to conduct a poll across those three countries: the United States, Great Britain and France. When asked 'Which foreign country do you prefer?', the United States topped the list in both Britain and France with 33 per cent and 26 per cent respectively. Second among the British was France with 22 per cent and the position was reciprocated in France with Britain a close second with 23 per cent. Across the Atlantic Britain was the preferred country with 43 per cent, followed by France with 11 per cent. When it came to the country which was liked least, Germany came top in the three countries, with 70 per cent among the French, 58 per cent among the Americans and 54 per cent among the British. Italy was a poor second overall with Russia in third place. The preferences of the British, the Americans and the French for one another's countries above others had its sources in history, in ties of blood and in the alliance of the First World War. The British and the French had some sympathies for Russia, partly because the idealism of the Russian revolution had not yet totally dissipated, partly because of Russia's actions in the Spanish Civil War and partly because of hopes of an alliance against Germany.

By the spring of 1939 Britain was preparing for war, though frantic efforts were being made to avoid it. In February 1939 the American institute stated that 69 per cent of Americans would wish their country to give all aid short of war to the British and French in the event of a war between them and the dictatorships. Such aid eventually came to Britain when she needed it most in 1940. In Britain 60 per cent of the public indicated that they were in favour of the government permitting Jewish settlement in the Holy Land. In March 70 per cent were not satisfied with air raid precautions as they knew them and wanted deep shelters. There was an expectation that should war break out, it would be followed immediately by massive bombing raids on centres of population. But even as the war clouds gathered the nation was still mixed up in its feelings.

Nearly half the public, both government and opposition supporters, saw Mr Chamberlain's policy of appeasement as one of buying time to rearm. But 42 per cent of government supporters felt that the policy would actually lead to peace, a view not shared by the opposition. Conversely, 43 per cent of the opposition supporters felt it was bringing war closer, a view little supported by government adherents. Nevertheless, Neville Chamberlain continued to have the support of about half the public throughout the period from October 1938 to March 1939, with 40 per cent opposed to him on average.

Russia had been cold-shouldered by the Western nations from the Revolution onwards, but the growth of German power was forcing a different view of events upon us. In March 84 per cent of the public wanted to see Britain and Russia being more friendly to each other and 87 per cent were in favour of a military alliance between Britain, France and Russia to try to contain Germany.

Questions were being asked about the ditching of Chamberlain as Prime Minister and in April Gallup reported that in such an event Anthony Eden (later Sir Anthony) was the favoured candidate with 38 per cent of the preferences, followed at a long distance by Lord Halifax and Winston Churchill, each with 7 per cent, although 36 per cent could not give an opinion on the subject. In that month news of government plans to conscript men for military service leaked out and there was a major shift of opinion towards the idea. Gallup's survey showed that 53 per cent preferred the army to consist of volunteers and 39 per cent were for conscription. Two weeks later the idea of conscription was approved by 58 per cent of the public.

By now the British Institute of Public Opinion was news. There were further articles in The *News Chronicle* explaining in detail the methods employed by our company, correspondence in *The Times* to which leading scientists all contributed, all because of the impact of this new barometer of public opinion, showing the support or lack of it for government measures, and the wishes and feelings of the public as war approached.

Meanwhile, another war had been going on for some years: the Japanese had been successfully attacking China. The British public were hostile to Japan, though they could not foresee that eventually they too would be drawn into war with that country. When asked in July how far Britain should go to defend her interests in China, 22 per cent were prepared to fight Japan if necessary, 37 per cent would forbid all trade with Japan and 17 per cent would supply money and arms to China.

By August many of the British were on their last summer holiday in peacetime. A recent Gallup survey had shown that six in ten of the British felt they could afford to go on holiday that year, and at least half of these preferred to go to the seaside. (A year later much of England's coastline would be denied to them and fortified against a possible invasion.) But the public did not feel too satisfied with Parliament adjourning on 4 August until 3 October. With the seriousness of the situation, and the decisions that might have to be taken, half the public wanted Parliament to be on hand. During this time the Western political initiative with Russia failed, the Russians and Germany invaded Poland, and Britain and France declared war on Germany.

The process of mobilisation continued, a small expeditionary force was sent to France, and a war cabinet was formed. Air raid precautions swung into action, gas masks were carried, and the children and some mothers were evacuated from the big cities to the country and the seaside. Poland was overrun from the east and west simultaneously without the Allies, who had guaranteed her territory, being able to lift a finger. Its triumph complete, Germany put out peace feelers claiming it had no real quarrel with the British Empire. The British waited for the expected aerial devastation, so often predicted, but, apart from the RAF departing for token raids on Germany, the skies remained clear. What was the mood of the British at this time, later known as the 'Phoney' War? Gallup took the initiative of a major survey of public opinion during the last week of the first month of the war (September). The public was in a determined mood. Asked 'Should we continue to fight till Hitler goes?' 89 per cent gave an unequivocal 'Yes'. Turning the question round, 77 per cent disapproved of discussing peace with Hitler, although a majority would have approved of discussions with the Germans if Hitler had been overthrown or replaced. This point was emphasised by a further question on whether their enemy was the German people or the Hitler government, to which 90 per cent replied 'Hitler's government'.

Comments from respondents showed, however, that many felt the German people were supporting Hitler or were tainted by the influence of Nazism. There were three distinct views of what the Hitler government meant. The first regarded it as a simple revival of German nationalism, with Hitler as another kind of Kaiser. The second saw Hitler as new, unique and abominable. The third group, who were more politically conscious, regarded it as a more complicated phenomenon posing an equally complicated problem of eradication in a future German society. The vast majority, 84 per cent, of those questioned were confident that we would win, but 4 per cent thought in terms of a stalemate, possibly with the images of the trenches of the Great War and the French Maginot Line in mind. Over half, 54 per cent, thought that the war would last less than three years and among them were many who were thinking in terms of a few months or 'being over by Christmas'. It was not necessarily foreseeable, then, that the war was to spread to involve every continent in the six years it took for it to come to its termination.

A remarkable feature of this survey was that the differences in responses from men and women were not great, nor were those from different social groups in the population. Certain differences that did emerge related to age, the older people being more aggressive and more confident and the younger more wary and more impressed by British failures and Nazi successes. People were anxious not only to give their replies but to add comments, all of which were recorded and which aided interpretation greatly. The general mood of the population was thus observed to be distinctly different from that expressed at the outset of the First World War, with far less overt patriotism and enthusiasm, but with somewhat more sober determination.

Questions directed to what was becoming known as the Home Front indicated some uncertainty and problems of transition from peace to war. There was criticism of the recently imposed censorship of news, and some slight concern abo t profiteering. At the same time, some industries were closing and others starting up, yet what complaints there were were more against retail traders than employers. Unemployment and poverty remained slightly exacerbated problems temporarily, although they would of course vanish as the nation became virtually totally mobilised. One important topic not so far mentioned in the survey referred to the only major act of war that had so far taken place - the almost simultaneous invasion of Poland by Russia and Germany. There was certainly some confusion about Russia's motives: 31 per cent thought that Russia's act had helped Germany, and 29 per cent thought that it hindered Germany, 12 per cent thought it had helped in the short term but hindered in the long run, 8 per cent thought she had acted in simple self interest, leaving a relatively high proportion, 20 per cent, of don't knows. Attitudes towards Russia were, of course, mixed, with a history of the Western allies trying to seek a last minute alliance with her but Russia preferring a deal with that most anti-communist country at that time, Nazi Germany. The British public's inability to evaluate this development is easily understandable.

Gallup continued to survey public attitudes in Britain throughout the war, although with increasing difficulty as staff and interviewers were called upon for war service. A poll at the beginning of November 1939 was on the subject of the war aims of the Allies, Britain and France. Forty-four per cent of the public felt that a declaration of what they were fighting for was needed, although 29 per cent thought that the war aims were already clear enough, and the remainder were against the idea or did not know. Again in November, government plans for food rationing became known, and Gallup reported that 60 per cent of the public were in favour of food rationing, 28 per cent thought it unnecessary at that time, and 12 per cent did not know.

Rationing did come into force on 8 January 1940. By this time many school children were evacuated away from the big cities. Asked if the evacuation of school chidren should be made compulsory the public gave a divided answer: 43 per cent said 'Yes', 46 per cent said 'No', and 11 per cent were uncertain. However, the government scheme by which parents paid up to a maximum of nine shillings (45p) per week for the upkeep of their evacuated school children was regarded as fair by 76 per cent of those asked.

By this time, Russia and Germany had carved up Poland between them, and Finland was under the threat of Russia. Gallup asked whether Britain should give military assistance to the Scandinavian countries if Russia should attack them. The answers divided: 42 per cent for military assistance, 38 per cent against, and 20 per cent did not know. In the event Russia did attack Finland; popular opinion in Britain was sympathetic to the Finns but nothing was done about it at that time. Russia was then by no means our ally and had just signed a non-aggression pact with Germany after the absorption of Poland. Gallup thought it worth while to ask the question whether Russia intended to give Germany help to defeat Britain and France or not. Only 14 per cent thought that this was her intention (or hoped so), and 68 per cent thought it was not at all her intention.

In December Gallup asked: 'Are you satisfied or dissatisfied with the government's conduct of the war?'. Just over three in five (61 per cent) were satisfied, 18 per cent were dissatisfied, 10 per cent did not know and the remaining 11 per cent took the opportunity to state that the war should stop. This is somewhat ironical since at that time none of the great battles of the war involving Britain itself had even begun. In addition to views about the government, the public had become more confident in Mr Chamberlain as Prime Minister. In the months before the war he received support from around 50 per cent of the public, but this increased to 68 per cent in November dropping slightly to 64 per cent in December. However, Mr Churchill was beginning to loom more importantly on the scene. He had been accepted into the Cabinet as First Lord of the Admiralty, and when asked, the public, given a hypothetical choice between Mr Chamberlain and Mr Churchill, voted 52 per cent for Mr Chamberlain and 30 per cent for Mr Churchill. Most of Churchill's support was from the opposition, a factor which led to his eventual acceptance as Prime Minister in 1940. In the same survey, a majority (57 per cent) regarded Nazi Germany, with whom we were at war, as the greatest threat to us compared with Soviet Russia, and 24 per cent thought that Soviet Russia was the greater threat. This was interpreted as being due to the proven military strength of Germany, and seemingly the incompetence of Russia in failing so far to defeat the tiny Finnish nation.

1940

On the home front, the question was still: 'When would the bombing start?'. A survey had shown that three-quarters of the population in likely target areas reckoned they could reach shelter from air raids within two or three minutes of the alarm siren sounding, a marked improvement from just before the war when the majority of people did not know where to go. On the other hand, although all the population had been issued with gas masks, by January 1940 only one in three people were actually carrying them as they went about their business.

Rationing had alerted the British people to the problem of food production, and in addition to the 17 per cent of people who grew some of their own food or kept livestock before the war, another 15 per cent had started to do so since. Gallup also reported that 30 per cent of people thought that the war would be over by the end of 1940, and 42 per cent between 1941 and 1943. In February three in four Britons approved of the help the British government was now sending Finland in their struggle against Russia, although only one in three would approve of sending British troops. In March 41 per cent felt that one day Britain would have to fight Russia, though 30 per cent rejected such an event. Approval of discussing peace proposals with Germany peaked at 29 per cent approving in February and was down to a mere 8 per cent by November.

By now the British were becoming acclimatised to the war environment, in particular to the blackout: 18 per cent of adults had suffered some injury, whether trivial or severe, in the course of the long dark winter. Meat rationing started in March, and Gallup discovered that 20 per cent of the population could not afford to buy their full allowance of rationed food at that time. Mr Chamberlain was losing popularity, and there was further speculation about his likely successor. Anthony Eden came first with 28 per cent of the votes in a Gallup survey, and Churchill second with 25 per cent. By May Chamberlain only had the support of 33 per cent of the public, as Denmark, Norway, Holland and Belgium succumbed to German invasion. Then in succession came the fall of France and the evacuation of the British army from Dunkirk. Winston Churchill now took over as Prime Minister.

By July, with the decisive Battle of Britain under way, 88 per cent of the public supported Churchill as Prime Minister - an unprecedented show of confidence which has never been surpassed by any other. Gallup took the occasion at the same time to disassociate itself from a government organisation, the war-time Social Survey set up by the Ministry of Information. The founding of this government body was a remarkable compliment to the impact of Gallup surveys on matters relating to the conduct of the war and the welfare of people. Just at that time an interesting example occurred. With the fall of France the possibility of German air raids had become so immediate that the prior policy of giving a general warning followed by an immediate warning of air raids was dropped. The public would have been constantly wondering whether to go to the air raid shelters or not. Instead, the warnings were confined to notifications of the danger of an immediate attack. The public approved of this new policy,

57 per cent agreeing and 38 per cent disagreeing. Further analysis showed that areas which had experienced bombing were more concerned to get a prior warning than those for whom it was still only a threat. The government wanted to exercise greater control over the press than it had done so far. Alerted to this, Gallup surveyed public opinion on the subject. Sixty-eight per cent of people thought that stricter controls on the press were unwise and only 19 per cent supported the idea. Much had been made in the press, both in Britain and in the United States, of the fact that even while Britain was at war, free comment and free institutions could still flourish in a democratic nation and were, even in those dark days, part and parcel of what Britain was fighting for.

By October 1940 80 per cent of the public felt that it was impossible for Germany to win the war solely by air attacks. The German blitz on London had started and 13 per cent of the public nationally were carrying a tin hat. Churchill's popularity had risen to 89 per cent of the public. He had succeeded in uniting the nation as no other man had, and the feeling that 'we were all in it together' was creating a new sense of community amongst people. An instance of this was shown in a Gallup Poll on awards and decorations for bravery or distinguished services. Should these be different for officers and men, or should this distinction be done away with? In November 60 per cent thought that any distinction should be done away with, and only 26 per cent thought they should be kept up.

With the blitz continuing, many people were living and sleeping in very unsatisfactory conditions, and fears were rising that disease, particularly diptheria, could become an epidemic. Gallup reported that 33 per cent of the public thought that innoculation against diseases like typhoid and diptheria should be free and compulsory, that 51 per cent thought innoculation should be free but not compulsory, and only 9 per cent regarded innoculation as not necessary.

The effect of this blitz on London and other cities was beginning to harden attitudes. At the end of 1940 52 per cent of the public regarded the German people themselves as their enemy, and 48 per cent the Nazi government as their enemy. Further, over two thirds of the public wanted more severe terms imposed on Germany after winning the war than had been done after the First World War. This is a measure of the British public's hostility rather than of their good sense: most informed people had followed Keynes in his demonstrated belief that the terms imposed upon Germany after the First World War had been so onerous that they broke up German democratic society. After the Second World War, as we know, substantial American aid was used to rebuild shattered European economies, including Germany's.

1941

At the beginning of the year the risk of invasion was still strongly present in the public mind. Sixty-two per cent thought that Germany would attempt an invasion during the year. The idea of making overtures for peace with Germany was rejected by 77 per cent of the public, and 82 per cent expected Britain to win the war. Sixty-two per cent also thought that Eire was wrong, in her own interests, in refusing the use of her naval ports to Britain.

By June satisfaction with Mr Churchill remained high at 87 per cent, although only 58 per cent were satisfied with the government's conduct of the war. There remained no support for peace proposals with Germany. Only 39 per cent thought that the Germans were intending to invade this country, and four out of five thought they would be defeated if they came. The idea of America coming into the war was mooted and 72 per cent thought this would happen. Opinions were divided about whether Britain could win without her.

Germany, abandoning the possible invasion of Britain, had invaded Russia in June. An August poll asked if this event had changed peoples' attitudes towards Russia, and only 27 per cent had been influenced. Russia by this time was a co-belligerent but not yet an ally. By October 49 per cent thought that Britain had not taken full advantage of the opportunities offered by this German attack. By November Gallup was asking whether the government should conscript women into the armed services, and the approvers (55 per cent) out-numbered the disapprovers (35 per cent). The emancipation of women had not gone so far as to persuade the British public that women should become fighting members of the armed services: two in three disapproved of this idea. Rationing was beginning to become rather tighter, and 43 per cent reported that they had difficulty in obtaining access to those foods which were still unrationed. But with the tightening of belts the question of a negotiated peace with Germany became even more unacceptable: 84 per cent disapproved of any idea of the government negotiating at that time. The public was more evenly divided in their replies to a question about declaring war on Vichy France: 38 per cent felt we should and 37 per cent thought we should not.

1942

By January Gallup was looking forward to the situation after the war. India had demanded self government and 31 per cent were for granting it during the war, outnumbered by the 41 per cent who wanted to wait until after the war (when in fact it came about). A huge proportion (86 per cent) of the public wanted to see Britain and Russia continuing to work together after the war. The goodwill towards the USSR at this time was immense, remembering that she was resisting the bulk of the German war effort and through this taking a great burden off the Western allies. When asked what was the most useful lesson Britain could learn from Russia's fight against Germany, almost one in four (23 per cent) said it was to deal drastically with slackers and racketeers, 15 per cent said it was national unity, and 14 per cent mentioned the thoroughness and determination of the Russian military command, particularly in guerrilla warfare.

With the attack on Pearl Harbor in December 1941, America was now in the war together with Britain and Russia. In July 1942 questions were posed about the Americans. At that time Russia was more popular than the United States with 62 per cent of people, while the United States was more popular with 24 per cent of people. Although only 6 per cent of Britons had visited the United States, 35 per cent of them knew Americans personally. There was clearly some distrust of the Americans coming into the war at the time that they did. Opinions were divided about whether the United States would want more than its fair share for helping to win the war, although the British did not think they would want more than their fair share of world markets after the war, or more than their fair share in deciding the peace terms. Again, opinions were divided about whether the Americans felt superior to the British, but the British did regard them as a more democratic people than themselves. The majority rejected the idea that the Americans were too willing to let other people fight for them. In the same survey 62 per cent of people felt that we should try to invade the continent of Europe that year. In a supplement to the survey, following the fall of Tobruk, only 35 per cent of the public were satisfied with the government's conduct of the war - the lowest point during the whole war - and approval of Mr Churchill dropped to 78 per cent. A little over one in two (55 per cent) said that they belonged to a national war savings group and 38 per cent said they had been called on at home to buy national savings stamps.

By the end of the year the mood of the British public, always positive since Churchill had taken over, had become even more optimistic. Thus, 48 per cent thought that Italy could be made to turn against Germany, although 29 per cent did not think that this was possible. In fact, the Italians did do just that. Eighty-eight per cent of the public approved of Churchill's statement that if Germany were beaten first, we should continue to fight until Japan were defeated. Approval of Mr Churchill reached 93 per cent in December. Again, looking forward to after the war, 46 per cent of the public would choose an alliance with America at the expense of Russia, and 32 per cent chose the opposite.

1943

By February 1943 the Allied armies, principally British and Commonwealth, had defeated the Italians and subsequently the Germans in North Africa. Invasion of somewhere in southern Europe was expected. Gallup asked whether the public thought the British army had already seen its hardest fighting, or did they think the hardest was still to come. Very rightly, 76 per cent thought that the hardest was yet to come, and it was indeed. Again, 76 per cent felt than an invasion of the Continent was necessary to defeat Germany. In March 67 per cent expected an Allied invasion of the Continent that year, although the June survey showed that very few people thought that the war would actually end that year. In that same month, Gallup returned to political affairs and asked its standard question about which party they would support if there were to be an election 'tomorrow'. A 10 per cent lead of Labour over the Conservatives emerged, together with support for a whole host of minor parties. This and other measurements of political preferences were hardly noticed during the war, which led to the supreme shock of the Labour victory towards its end.

Later surveys in 1943 dealt with many miscellaneous matters seemingly irrelevant now, but a few indications are of interest. In August 84 per cent approved of the bombing of Rome, although it was declared an open city subsequently, avoiding much damage. In November, talk of the Germans' secret weapon was rife, and Gallup sounded public opinion on the point. Fifty-nine per cent thought it was a bluff, and 21 per cent felt that it was true. The following year was to prove this minority correct, with the V1 and V2 rocket attacks on south east England.

1944

By the beginning of this year, the question was not whether the war would be won, but when it would be won. Already, seven in ten were agreeing with the Russian proposal that Germany would have to help to rebuild the countries they had destroyed. Gallup also asked about the advisability of a general election. A minority (12 per cent) thought it should be held within the next few months, and the majority (82 per cent) felt it should be held as soon as Germany was defeated, or, at most, within twelve months of their defeat. In February Gallup again reported a Labour lead over the Conservatives. The following month the public was evenly divided on whether or not the three main parties were right to agree not to fight each other at war-time by-elections. The government were taking steps to deal with reconstruction in Britain after the war, and the public were asked how satisfied they were with the progress reported: 43 per cent were satisfied, 35 per cent being dissatisfied. Around one in four (27 per cent) said that they would like a temporary prefabricated house, being erected to relieve the housing shortage, though 31 per cent wanted to wait longer for a more permanent home. Approval of the government's conduct of the war was high at 75 per cent, and it rose to 80 per cent in June, the month of the invasion of Europe.

Gallup asked in July about the idea of a National Health Service, and received 55 per cent approval of it as against 32 per cent who wished to keep things as they were. The idea of health centres rather than the conventional doctor's surgery was approved of by 69 per cent of the public. (The National Health Service did come about, but the health centres have only come about sporadically, even after many years of peace.) Even during war-time the public had a cynical view of their politicians. Although 36 per cent thought that they were trying to do their best for the country, 22 per cent saw them as having their party mainly in mind, and 35 per cent thought they were out merely for themselves.

In August Gallup was asking about the effects of the flying bombs (the V1s). Half the British public thought that they were more trying than the blitz of three years before, and 31 per cent thought that they were less trying. Attitudes to Germany remained as hard as ever, with 76 per cent of the public demanding unconditional surrender. By September a whole survey was devoted to Germany after the war. Virtually everyone thought that the chief Nazis should be punished, mostly by execution. Other Germans who had committed crimes should be tried by the United Nations (66 per cent). Nearly nine in ten thought that Germany should be forced to make good the war damage she had done to other countries, and the idea of drafting German men to repair war damage seemed perfectly acceptable to most people. The splitting up of Germany permanently into a number of smaller German states was approved of by 56 per cent and disapproved of by 23 per cent. There were more mixed feelings about giving portions of German territory to other countries, but the idea of giving parts of eastern Germany, including East Prussia to Poland was approved of. (Actually East Prussia became part of the Soviet Union.) Two in three felt that the whole industrial area of the Ruhr and Rhineland should be taken away from Germany permanently and made into an international zone, although this did not come about. That Germany should be totally disarmed was almost unanimously approved.

1945

By January 1945 Germany was defending on all fronts and Gallup asked if the present war was the last world war or was another war likely during the next 25 years. The British public was surprisingly cynical, 28 per cent thinking it was the last world war, but 48 per cent expecting another. The twenty-five years mentioned then have since passed, and although the world has not been free from war in some quarter at any time, world war has been avoided so far. By February although satisfaction with Mr Churchill remained high at 85 per cent and with the government's conduct of the war at 77 per cent, there was again a great deal of support for Labour. Thirty-three per cent thought that the next government would be a Labour government, and only 22 per cent thought it would be a Conservative one. Labour had a lead in voting intentions of 18 per cent over the Conservatives at this time, with the rest nowhere. By April voters were being asked if they had checked their names on the electoral register and only one in four had done so by that time. Labour still had a lead in voting intentions and there was some support for continuing the coalition government after the election. The most important issues, as Gallup reported in May, were housing (41 per cent) and full employment (15 per cent), followed by a list of problems including some of the ones needing to be solved in the transition from war to peace, such as demobilisation, treatment of the occupied countries, and food rationing. Gallup's June survey included a question on the best party to handle the housing question and this turned out to be Labour (42 per cent), Conservatives (25 per cent) and Liberals (13 per cent). These preferences were clearly on party lines. The predominance of housing as an issue related first to the cessation of house building throughout virtually six years, though the population was growing and had expectations of a better life, and secondly to the destruction wrought by the blitz in major cities and the later flying bomb attacks on the south east.

Gallup's was a lone voice in the 1945 General Election as no other research company was operating at that time. Its methods were validated on a national scale for the first time by the results. Two items slightly blur the comparison. Gallup did not poll in Northern Ireland, where party allegiances are on different party lines, and did not survey the armed forces, who voted from all over the world. It is generally considered that Gallup's accuracy was within 2 per cent. Politicians, hitherto sceptical, began to pay more attention to Gallup findings. An interesting corollary to the results was the idea, put forward by the losers, that it was the armed forces' vote that had lost them the election could not be sustained in view of what Gallup showed about voting at home.

2 1945-1951 : Labour's First Term

The Labour government came into power on 26 July 1945. The British electorate who had granted them an overwhelming victory were in a situation unprecedented in the history of these islands. The war which had started with a series of defeats, temporarily stalemated by the Battle of Britain, had gone on to involve nearly all the world. Victory in Europe after a series of advances on all fronts was less than three weeks behind, and successive naval and land victories in the Pacific spelt out the inevitable defeat of Japan. Also unprecedented was Labour's sweeping victory, giving them for the first time an absolute majority in the House of Commons of 146 over the Conservatives, Liberals and all others combined. This gave Labour power to do anything a British government of the time could do. The limitations on its power were not in the House, but in the external world. During the war Britain had lost something like a quarter of its wealth, amounting to about £7 billion. Having exhausted its foreign exchange early on, the funding of the British war machine and the feeding of its citizens had been largely financed by American lease-lend, which came to an abrupt end in August 1945.

The National Debt had increased, the purchasing power of the pound had declined. The housing stock had been seriously affected by air-raid destruction and six years of virtual stagnation in house building and repairs. The demobilisation of the armed forces put enormous pressures upon accommodation as they returned to their families and private lives. New political structures in Europe, the colonies and elsewhere in the world, would need the government's attention and would occupy its time. Against all this, Labour was committed to a massive housing programme, the provision of welfare and medical services according to need and a programme of nationalisation of major industries, all put forward in terms of social justice rather than as revolutionary ideology. Gallup's first post-election poll in July indicated the mood of the country. The election had been brought about rather more by the falling apart of what consensus among politicians there was than by popular demand, since, when asked, 58 per cent of the electorate thought it had been a bad thing for the country to hold an election at that time and only 28 per cent regarded it as a good thing. Nevertheless, the public saw Labour as intending to carry out what it had promised.

Its policy was seen as introducing sweeping changes such as nationalisation (56 per cent) rather than governing along the existing lines but more effectively (30 per cent). The election itself left some scars. There were criticisms in retrospect of the way the election had been fought - 41 per cent approved and 42 per cent disapproved of the way parties had conducted their campaigns. One in three of the disapprovers thought heckling and mudslinging had been an undesirable feature of the campaign. The most urgent problem on the Home Front (wartime phrases were still in use) that the government should turn its attention to was considered by 63 per cent to be housing. One in three (32 per cent) said that they were looking for fresh accommodation.

The war in the East came to a most dramatic end with the dropping of atomic bombs on Hiroshima and Nagasaki. Within a few days, on 14 August, Japan unconditionally surrendered to the Allies. The most destructive war ever was over and peoples' minds turned to peace. But the new and terrible weapon has influenced the thinking of the military, politicians, religious leaders and the public ever since. In a survey immediately after the war ended, one in two (52 per cent) thought that the existence of the atomic bomb would make future wars less likely, compared with 12 per cent who thought they would be more likely, with the remainder feeling that the bomb would have no effect or were undecided about it. In the same survey 51 per cent agreed that each country should abolish its armed forces and replace them with an international force under world government, although 29 per cent disagreed with this. Plans were being laid for the formation of the United Nations Organisation and this survey question may have reflected the optimism about the part it would eventually play. Nevertheless, power politics were still with us and the United States of America was thought by 38 per cent of Britons to be the most influential country in world affairs over the next five years, followed by Russia (31 per cent) and Britain (14 per cent). These three countries had in fact the only substantial armies in the world at this time: Britain's in particular by wartime conscription which was continuing. Conscription in peacetime for young men was approved of by 65 per cent of the electorate, with 27 per cent disapproving.

Early soundings on the Labour government were favourable, but were never to be as positive in subsequent years. In August 56 per cent of the public stated their satisfaction with Mr Attlee as Prime Minister, although in an open question as to who they would prefer to lead the new government after the war, Anthony Eden topped the list with 31 per cent, followed by Winston Churchill (20 per cent) and Attlee, the actual Prime Minister, gaining only 4 per cent. In October a majority (57 per cent) approved of the government's record, though it could hardly be said to have got into its stride yet in so few months, and it was not to obtain majority approval at any other point in its career. On the other hand, only 29 per cent in late September felt that the government was telling the public enough about the policies it was following

The cancellation of lease-lend by President Truman within a few days of the defeat of Japan came as a shock to an economy that was not geared up for it. It caused resentment towards the United States, as shown in the answers to a question put in September on how attitudes towards our allies had changed since the year before. A little under one in two (46 per cent) said their attitude towards the United States had not changed, but around one in three (35 per cent) said they had become less friendly. As far as attitudes to Russia were concerned, 54 per cent said their attitudes were unchanged, while the remainder were almost evenly balanced between those becoming more friendly and those becoming less friendly, with one in ten undecided.

By November there was some pessimism: 55 per cent thought that shortages were greater than the year before, and 52 per cent thought it likely that there would be a wave of strikes in the coming months. Accommodation was still a problem and two in three agreed with Mr Bevan's, the Housing Minister, proposal to requisition any part of houses that were not in use. Despite the problems being faced, Labour was determined to change the face of Britain and had already announced a programme to nationalise the Bank of England, the coal industry and civil aviation. By the end of 1945 95 per cent had heard about these plans for nationalisation and 59 per cent approved of them. Nationalisation involved compensation, and the extent of this, both in principle and in relation to any economic difficulties, provoked controversy in Labour's ranks. By the end of the year Britain had succeeded in negotiating a loan, under stringent conditions, from the United States, whose terms were somewhat resented.

1946

In January Gallup reported that 70 per cent of the public thought that this American loan was acceptable. Could we do without it? Forty-seven per cent thought we could not, although 32 per cent thought that by keeping up an austerity programme we might reconstruct our industry and trade without borrowing. The extent to which consumption was controlled by rationing and the acceptance of it seems amazing, viewed in the perspective of the eighties. In April, with the first year of peace coming to an end, 39 per cent approved of giving extra rations for Victory Day party celebrations but 56 per cent disapproved of this. Bread rationing, which had been successfully avoided during the war, was now put forward as a necessary measure during peacetime and only 41 per cent approved of this versus 50 per cent against the idea. Further, 51 per cent said it would work and a substantial minority of 35 per cent said it wouldn't. At that time, just over five pounds of bread was the average reasonable weekly ration. Despite this, at least some of the population were prepared to accept further food restrictions in order to help those worse off than themselves. Almost one in two, for example, approved of trying to help India (47 per cent) or Allied countries (43 per cent). A minority (18 per cent) were even prepared to help ex-enemy countries, though three in four disapproved of such help.

Britain was showing signs of thinking like a Third World country nowadays: the most urgent problem on the domestic front was now food shortages (mentioned by 42 per cent), displacing housing, 31 per cent compared with 61 per cent the previous January. Around a half (51 per cent) said that the quality of food was worse than the year before, 40 per cent the same, and only 9 per cent thought it was any better. Nevertheless, the vast majority was managing, perhaps with some difficulty, on the bread ration. Food rationing, although inconvenient and boring, was largely accepted in the egalitarian spirit of the time. So was the broad concept of the Welfare State, and the first steps came about with the National Insurance Act of 1946, with protection against sickness or unemployment and allowances for children. A National Health Service was eventually introduced in 1948. By April 1946 65 per cent thought it would result in better health services for the country as a whole, and only 20 per cent thought this would not happen.

The Conservative party was beginning to recover from the psychological shock of its defeat in 1945. The electorate, although still regarding Churchill as a great leader and as the most admired person at the time, had rejected his party. Further, in the electoral campaign, the Conservative party had played at least lip service to many egalitarian reforms that the Labour government was actually introducing, in consequence that in opposition they were unable to reject the principles, but could only attack on lesser matters such as the wisdom, costs or tactics of Labour's actions. In August only a minority (29 per cent) thought that a Conservative government would return in five years and 48 per cent thought that this would not happen. In fact, this was to come about. In contrast, 46 per cent thought the Tories would return within ten years and only 24 per cent not. Two months later dissatisfaction with Labour was being expressed in other ways. Although Labour was making efforts to build houses, it was beset with both material and financial shortages. So only 36 per cent thought that the authorities were doing everything possible to relieve the housing shortage and a majority, 56 per cent, thought Labour was not doing so. Some aspects of the nationalisation programme were also becoming distinctly controversial. On whether nationalisation should be carried out in two major fields - road transport and gas and electricity - the replies were a narrow vote against the nationalisation of the former - 37 per cent thinking it should and 46 per cent thinking it should not - and the reverse for gas and electricity: 48 per cent and 35 per cent respectively.

An interesting Gallup finding in that year was that 50 per cent of the public thought that we had a democracy in Britain, and 32 per cent not. Whether the third who thought not were thinking principally in terms of the persistence of war time controls over all manner of activities, or whether they saw the Labour majority as rendering the opposition impotent, was not investigated. When the question was repeated forty years later, 65 per cent thought that Britain was democratic, while 23 per cent took the opposite view.

1947

The year opened with the nationalisation of the coal industry, followed by a freeze-up which was to last three months, produce great demands on heating and hamper the country's transport to the point of partial paralysis. Twenty-six per cent of the public had made New Year resolutions to cut down smoking. This was probably due more to cost and possible social reasons since neither the medical profession nor the public were aware then of its long-term, possibly lethal, damage to health. There were mixed feelings about food rations. Compared to six months before food was assessed in three ways: in terms of quantity, quality and variety. On quantity the public felt that food had got worse, quality was just about the same as six months' earlier, and it was felt that there was more variety. So although neither the quantity nor quality of the food available was improving at least there was a tendency to find it more interesting. In the following month 60 per cent found it was harder to make ends meet than a year before. The great freeze was having its effect: 63 per cent were for the introduction of fuel rationing - although now coal belonged to the people they weren't getting enough of it - but 34 per cent felt that voluntary restraint might be enough. The economic facts of life were beginning to sink in - that production must increase before wages went up was accepted by 69 per cent of the electorate. In this context, 66 per cent agreed that 'piece work' (payment by results achieved rather than by the hour) was likely to increase production. Nevertheless, only 50 per cent approved of the piece work concept with 30 per cent disapproving. In those days piece work was thought to create dissent and envy on the shop floor, but, with the subsequent increase in mechanisation and even automation, this controversy has largely died away. There is even some irony in the discussion of this subject at this time, since due to the fuel shortage factories had to shut, creating temporary unemployment.

The spirit of unity and common purpose that had carried the British through the war might be said to be weakening. In April 61 per cent thought that the black market (principally food, petrol and clothes) was increasing and 65 per cent thought that the authorities should be taking stronger measures to combat it. What had been thought to have been simply unpatriotic during the war appeared not so heinous in peace time. In the same study 48 per cent thought that family life was less successful than it had been in their parents' generation, although 22 per cent thought that family life was more successful and 17 per cent felt it was the same as ever. Despite this, later in the year (July) 40 per cent of the public had someone in their family deliberately giving up some of their rations to help the others, for the most part Mum. So at least here sense of family was as strong as ever.

By July the American loan negotiated in Labour's first year and destined to finance Britain's economic recovery through until 1951 was exhausted. Britain was in a crisis with the balance of payments problems, lack of foreign currency, disappointing production, increases in costs of materials purchased abroad and the high costs of maintaining Britain's presence in Germany. As an expression of dissatisfaction, the Conservatives were ahead of Labour for the first time by 3 per cent in August. In the following month 98 per cent of the public were aware of an economic crisis and 75 per cent thought it was really serious. There was resentment against the United States, with 57 per cent thinking it likely that America would want a say in running Britain's affairs before she would help us further. If this were to be the case, 51 per cent said we should reject American help. At this time there was a recrudescence of fascism, with heavily orchestrated public meetings in London, although it was to peter out of its own accord. In October Gallup found that only one in four (28 per cent) of the public thought fascists should be allowed the basic right of free speech, and 57 per cent, possibly including many still deeply shocked by revelations about the Nazi death camps, thought that they should be denied this right.

One the the few happy public events of the year was the marriage of Princess Elizabeth, the present Queen, to Philip on 20 November. This was widely covered by the media and diverted peoples' minds from daily life for a little while. The public approved of the wedding arrangements in the main, with 50 per cent thinking that they were just right, 13 per cent thinking they were too simple, but 29 per cent thinking they were too elaborate. The last figure is probably more an indication of the austerity of the times than of any anti-Royalist sentiment. The Royal Family was, and is, perceived differently from the aristocracy. In the same survey, 32 per cent thought that the power of the House of Lords should be reduced, 5 per cent thought it should be increased and 45 per cent left alone. Fifty-six per cent wanted to abolish the right of sons of peers to inherit their parents' seats in the Lords and only 26 per cent wished to retain this. As far as the Commons was concerned, the Conservative party at 50.5 per cent in terms of voting intentions against Labour's 38 per cent (November) was at its highest point in support and Labour at its lowest in the whole of that Parliament. This was probably due to the hardships of the time and dissatisfaction with the fruits of victory, and the fact that although most of Labour's plans for nationalisation and other reforms had passed into Acts of Parliament or were taking shape, any beneficial results from them would inevitably be slow to realise.

1948

Exactly a year after nationalising coal, the State took over the rail network under the name of British Rail on 1 January. It would be electricity's turn in April and gas a month later. The public was beginning to have mixed feelings about this. Gallup's first poll that year showed that 49 per cent thought the nationalisation of coal had been a success, 20 per cent a failure and 14 per cent thought it had had no effect. Views on transport were less positive: 33 per cent thought that nationalisation would be successful, 29 per cent a failure, and 7 per cent as having no effect. As for the future nationalisation of iron and steel, 31 per cent thought it should be done, 36 per cent thought it should not be carried out and 33 per cent could not decide. This last industry was to become a shuttlecock between successive governments. In contrast, the majority of the public (61 per cent) thought that the new Health Service was a good thing and only 13 per cent a bad thing (February). It was to come into being in July 1948, but the Health Minister, Aneuran Bevan, was currently in dispute with the medical profession over money and status. In the same survey 64 per cent had heard of this dispute and 30 per cent sided with the doctors and 28 per cent were against them. In a survey in October of that year the National Health Service came out as the best thing the government had done since

1945, with the top score of 35 per cent. Nationalisation, in general, was considered to be the worst by 20 per cent.

Again, in May, the public was sounded about the problems the government should solve. The list looks alarming. The top item was the cost of living (mentioned by 38 per cent and rising to 51 per cent in the following months), housing (31 per cent), food and food rationing (21 per cent) and clothes rationing (14 per cent). The new allocation of clothing coupons was about to be issued, and when they were 35 per cent stated that they were spending them then, but 54 per cent stated that they were waiting for prices to fall, an indication of the pressure of the cost of living. But there was a distinctly new mood. The Americans had finally recognised that the restoration of the European economies, although presented as an act of charity to the American public, was as much in their interest as it was in Europe's. Britain was receiving a substantial allocation of Marshall Aid as it was called, and it would be spent more wisely than previous injections of American money. There was caution about it: 23 per cent thought that the Marshall Plan would have a big effect on our standard of living, and 42 per cent little effect.

By the late summer things were getting a little easier in some things. Both potato and bread rationing had ended, for instance. Yet in July disapprovers of Mr Attlee as Prime Minister outnumbered approvers by 49 per cent to 40 per cent. In contrast there was substantial majority approval of Mr Bevan as Foreign Secretary. The Conservatives had a 7 point lead over Labour in voting support and there was dissatisfaction expressed with the government's performance by 54 per cent as against 36 per cent satisfied. In the next month 59 per cent said that they found it harder than 6 months before to make ends meet, compared with only 6 per cent finding it easier. In the same survey the public was asked what should be the weekly wage or weekly income on which a young couple should get married and the average of the answers was £6.

The Labour government was now more pre-occupied with running the country, with the implementation of its various reforms, and generally trying to cope than progressing any further in terms of socialist ideology. The National Health Service was gradually coming into being and by August nine out of ten people had registered with a National Health Service doctor, with only a tiny minority reporting any difficulty in arranging this. By October 38 per cent of the public reported that they had used one of the services of the National Health scheme, these users divided as 35 per cent being satisfied with the treatment they received and only 3 per cent dissatisfied in some way. An October survey showed that the most urgent domestic problems were food supplies (26 per cent), housing (18 per cent) and the cost of living (12 per cent). Fifty-nine per cent stated that they were unable to put any money away in any form of saving, yet 57 per cent did manage to have a summer holiday away from home that year.

Conscription in peacetime was alien to the tradition of the Labour party, yet the government had passed an Act which meant that it came into being on 1 January 1949. The reasons were related largely to Britain's obligations as an occupying power and a keeper of the peace. It was to remain for a decade until an effective nuclear force was put forward as a substitute for a large army. The British public were on the whole for it: 57 per cent thought that it should be continued and 33 per cent that it should be stopped.

1949

The government was now in its fourth year and had to go to the country in the middle of 1950. Both the government, the opposition and the general public began to turn its mind to both the timing of and the possible outcome of the forthcoming election. In January Winston Churchill, who had been less incisive in Opposition than he had as a war leader, was still regarded as the favourite to lead a possible Conservative government. Then the Conservatives led Labour in popular support by 44 per cent to 40.5 per cent, at a time when a slight majority of the electorate were dissatisfied rather than satisfied with the government. The Labour government was thought to have been too socialist by 43 per cent, not socialist enough by 13 per cent and about right by 31 per cent. The dissatisfaction with government progress in housing was expressed by 61 per cent of the public, and further nationalisation was becoming a dirty word. The government's plan to nationalise the iron and steel industry was disapproved of by 51 per cent and only approved of by 28 per cent. As for a government proposal to take over the pubs in the New Towns, 48 per cent disapproved of it against 22 per cent approving, and there was majority disapproval of the possibility of the government nationalising breweries and pubs across the country. Things were easier, however. Sweets were derationed, that is, free and available for sale. Before all this, in March, indications were that people would tend to buy more sweets, but once they became freely available a majority found that they were unable to obtain as many sweets as when they had been rationed and not only disapproved of the de-rationing but thought that they should be put back on ration, which did occur. So this was one of the few government controls that the public was prepared to put up with.

In the main there was a reaction against the general extent of government control over many aspects of life, and in July, when discussing what cuts the government should make in its expenditure, 52 per cent put forward the size of the Civil Service. Second came the armed services, a mere 15 per cent, and third food subsidies at 8 per cent. It was in August that the government suffered a serious financial and psychological shock, that of having to devalue sterling from $4.03, a level at which it had stood since before the war, to $2.80. This was seen as for what it was - a false devaluation and therefore a defeat. Forty years later the British public was to view the movement of currencies against one another with a great deal more equanimity. Virtually everybody had heard about the devaluation by November that year, 44 per cent thought that its effects were likely to be bad as against 21 per cent thinking it would be good, and 74 per cent thought that prices were likely to go up as a result. As a consequence a number of cuts in public expenditure, including education and housing among others, had to be announced in October, together with the charge of a shilling (5p) for prescriptions under the National Health Service, originally designed to be totally free. This last policy was received with mixed feelings, 51 per cent agreeing with the shilling charge and 44 per cent against it.

The year closed with the government distinctly unpopular and trailing the Conservatives by 4 per cent in voting intentions. But in December Gallup asked some questions of the public about life in general. The British people were thought to be better off in health (by 51 per cent as against worse by 20 per cent), getting better in intelligence (by 42 per cent as against 20 per cent worse), yet from the point of view of moral conduct, only 10 per cent thought we were getting better and 58 per cent worse. There was also a tendency to think that, in terms of inner happiness, things were tending to get worse rather than better.

1950

Labour called the election for February 1950. The government had lasted four-and-a-half years, had transformed major aspects of British society, and held the economy together. In foreign policy it had had to deal with a vastly changed world and new international structures. It was becoming physically and intellectually exhausted, and while the electorate was not too disenchanted altogether, it lacked enthusiasm. Gallup's studies of the election again reflected the general position and again the Northern Ireland seats slightly interfered with the comparison, but for Britain itself Gallup's estimate was considered to be within 2 points of the result. The relatively small gains in the Conservative vote at the expense of Labour produced a dramatic effect on the seats won, as only the British system can. Instead of an absolute majority of 146, the new Labour government had to make do with 5. The month following the election the electorate appeared to be aware of the difficulties governing the situation, since 46 per cent of them wanted to see another General Election in the near future, and slightly more (42 per cent) felt that the government should co-operate with the opposition rather than pursue an independent policy (40 per cent).

Throughout the year dissatisfaction continued to be felt with circumstances of life in general, the old subjects of housing and the cost of living still high in the public mind along with the problems of still rationed food. Nevertheless in May, when asked to compare their present family circumstances with what life was like as a child, 56 per cent thought that they were better off than their father had been, 14 per cent the same, and 25 per cent worse off. In August, after the start of the Korean War, the British public seemed to be prepared to shoulder increasing burdens. More than three in four (78 per cent) of them agreed with increased government spending on defence and 61 per cent agreed that this would imply cuts in the standard of living. By October, continuing its policy of controlling the commanding heights of the economy, Labour's plans for the nationalisation of iron and steel were known. Gallup took the opportunity to review public attitudes towards nationalisation in general and in particular their views of the proposed nationalisation of iron and steel, and the possible nationalisation of five other industries. Between one in four and one in three approved of the nationalisation of iron and steel (32 per cent), insurance (31 per cent), chemicals (27 per cent), and cement (26 per cent), with around one in two disapproving in each case. Approval was even lower for the nationalisation of sugar (25 per cent) and of meat (22 per cent) with three in five disapproving. The majority of the public seemed to be against any further nationalisation. How did they view industries already nationalised? Only the National Health Service commanded overwhelming support - 71 per cent thinking nationalisation had been good in its case - and it has largely survived in its original form until the present day. Emotional support for the miners may well have accounted for the support there was for the nationalisation of coal, but the other services did not meet any kind of majority approval. Coal was, on balance, viewed positively, with 45 per cent thinking nationalisation had been a good thing and 39 per cent thinking it had been bad. On the three others, the balance of opinion was negative, with only 33 per cent thinking the nationalisation of gas and electricity had been a good thing, 30 per cent for the railways, and 26 per cent for road transport.

1951

The government put forward the idea of a Festival of Britain, celebrating British achievement, in London in 1951. By late 1950 nearly half of the population had thought of visiting the coming Festival, and having regard to the accommodation shortage, Gallup also found that nearly a third would be prepared to put up visitors to this exhibition should they arrive. But with the Korean War continuing and difficulties at home the wisdom of such public expenditure was being questioned by February 1951. Nevertheless, 58 per cent thought it should be proceeded with, and it did in fact come about during May-September, the last months of the Labour government.

Three in five (58 per cent) of the public in January felt that there was much danger of world war and the same proportion felt that if it did come about it would be likely to arise through Russia, while 21 per cent thought America would be to blame. In the event, however, of a war against Russia, the balance of opinion was that the British people would be less willing to fight than they had been against Nazi Germany. As far as the conflict in Korea was concerned, around one in two thought that we should stop fighting, while one in four wanted to fight on. The British public's opinion of General MacArthur was not particularly flattering: a little over one in four thought that he was doing a good job but two in five gave him a negative rating. Naturally, therefore, a majority (55 per cent) approved in May of President Truman's dismissal of MacArthur, and at the same time almost three in four felt that the best thing to do in Korea was to confine the fighting to the peninsular, though one in ten wanted to extend it into China. Given these findings, it was hardly surprising that two months later four in five of the public said that the United Nations' agreement to peace talks was a good thing.

Economic difficulties and the Korean War led to a severe Budget in April. Despite the reasonable rating of the Prime Minister - 49 per cent for, versus 40 per cent against - it was not particularly popular. False teeth and glasses would have to be paid for under a new scheme and 59 per cent disapproved of this measure. This led to the resignation of the Health Minister, Aneuran Bevan, along with two others, Wilson and Freeman. Since both Mr Bevan and Stafford Cripps had resigned on grounds of health, the government itself was weakened considerably. In the first four months of the year, the Conservatives registered substantial leads (up to 14.5 per cent in the Gallup surveys), compared with a narrow single point advantage for Labour in the previous December. A majority, 54 per cent, in January were in favour of another General Election, and by March the Conservatives were the public's favourites to win the next one.

Also, Eden was the public's choice as Prime Minister if the Conservatives did win the election, closely followed by Churchill. In the event, the October election was nowhere near so clear cut. Labour obtained more votes than the Conservatives but won fewer seats. Gallup's final survey, although statistically accurate, suggested that the Conservatives would obtain the greater number of votes in Britain - it was that close.

3 1951-1957 : The Road to Suez

Ironically, foreign affairs were thought to be the most urgent problem the government must solve in its first few months - with Egypt and Korea looming large on the horizon - followed by one of Britain's long-term post-war problems, inflation. Two in three of the public approved of the government's attitude in the dispute with Egypt, and slightly more, seven in ten, felt that Egypt should not be allowed to take over the Sudan. On the home front, a little over one in three thought that unemployment would increase over the next six months, compared with fewer than one in ten who saw the problem diminishing. Three in five said that compared with six months before they were finding it harder to make ends meet, and the same proportion thought that prices would go up in the following six months.

In that same December survey, one in two of the public thought that the new 'zebra' crossings were an improvement, but one in five felt otherwise. Looking forward to Christmas, three in five were going to have poultry, one in two a family party, and two in five were having a Christmas tree. Slightly more (44 per cent) said that they would be filling children's stockings, while one in ten were spending the festive season away from home.

1952

That economic times would be difficult in the new year was recognised by the public early on in January, with 52 per cent accepting as inevitable the government's warning that the Budget was likely to be a stiff one, though one in three felt that it could be avoided. At the same time, 77 per cent expected prices to rise over the next 6 months, compared with 60 per cent just a month earlier. It perhaps was not surprising that Labour was ahead in the public's affections: by 3.5 points in voting intentions and 6 points as the party who would do the best job 'in looking after people like yourself'. Despite this Labour advantage, however, 62 per cent of the public thought that the Budget was a fair one - a figure to be only rarely surpassed in the following years. A week later, though, this figure had dropped to 50 per cent, with 37 per cent seeing it as an unfair Budget.

In foreign affairs, the British public was still adopting an insular attitude, with around two in three wanting the army to remain British, compared with the one in five who thought it should become part of a European army. Naturally, 45 per cent thought it would be better for Britain if Eisenhower, allied supreme commander in Europe, stayed in his job rather than becoming President of the USA. Aneurin Bevan's views on Russia, Britain's ally just a few years earlier, did not strike a particularly responsive note with the public: one in two siding with other Labour leaders, against one in five siding with Bevan. They disagreed with him, for example, that war was more likely to come from world economic conditions rather than from Soviet military ambitions, and also with his claim that the Russian military menace was not really as great as some people said. The public was, however, almost evenly balanced on Bevan personally, slightly more thinking he was sincere than saw him as being mainly prompted by personal ambition. In March 60 per cent approved of Britain making her own atom bomb, at a time when the public was taking a critical view of the United States. While 37 per cent approved of the role the United States was playing in world affairs, 34 per cent disapproved. On the other hand, 72 per cent disapproved of the Soviet Union's role.

In April Gallup conducted a major study into the public's attitudes towards the institution of marriage. That marriages were less successful than in earlier years was rejected by the 43 per cent who thought that the higher divorce rate was a function of divorce being easier; 26 per cent accepted the view that marriages were less successful than in their grandparents' days. Asked to rate their own marriage with their parents', 85 per cent saw their own as successful compared with 79 per cent for their parents'. Overall, 31 per cent rated their marriage as more successful than their parents' marriage, twice as many as thought it had been less successful. The highest ratings came from men, senior citizens, people married in a church, and people who had been engaged for more than two years.

When asked to rate the importance of various things in contributing to a successful marriage, three were mentioned by 70 per cent or more as being 'very important': mutual respect and appreciation (78 per cent), understanding and tolerance (76 per cent), and regular or adequate income (70 per cent). At the bottom of the list was agreement on politics, with only 6 per cent seeing this as 'very important'. The survey also included one of Gallup's long-term, more profound questions: the ideal size of a family. Four per cent thought that the ideal size of a family was father, mother and fewer than two children. Eleven times as many, 43 per cent, gave two children as their ideal number, 25 per cent mentioned three children, and 26 per cent four or more. While 21 per cent of young adults, aged under 21, gave this latter number of children, the proportion mentioning four or more rose to 33 per cent among senior citizens.

It might surprise some readers of the late 1980s that 35 years earlier, only a bare majority, 53 per cent, of British adults agreed that a wife should be legally entitled to a fixed share of her husband's income. A little over one in three, 36 per cent, including one in two men, disagreed with the idea. Apart from petty things, money was the thing most couples said they quarrelled about. In 1948, four years earlier, people had been asked what was the best age for getting married. Twenty-five was the average ideal age for men and 23 for women: the same ages for each sex given in 1952 as the actual age at which they got married. In only 11 per cent of the cases was the wife older than her husband. On the question of engagements, one in two preferred short engagements, while one in three preferred long engagements. Short engagements were the majority view among women, people aged under 50, married couples, and couples who gave the highest rating to the success of their own marriage.

When asked how much a week a couple should have before getting married, the average amount given was £7.17s (£7.85p) or a little over £400 a year. On other problems of marriage, a little over one in four said that they would have welcomed more advice on all the problems involved, though three in five either felt that they already knew enough or didn't welcome such advice. A question of perhaps even greater significance in the age of AIDS was whether a medical certificate should be produced showing that neither party to a marriage had VD. Then, two in three felt that it should be a requirement.

On the question of divorce, substantial majorities of the public agreed with the then present grounds: desertion (88 per cent), cruelty (88 per cent), adultery (84 per cent), and insanity (79 per cent). Two in three thought that it should be possible to automatically get a divorce when both parties wanted it, though only one in three felt that either party should have the right to get a divorce irrespective of the wishes of the other. Around two in three also approved of everyone having to see somebody like the Marriage Guidance Council to try to mend matters, before going to the divorce courts. Slightly fewer, around one in two, agreed with the concepts that:

- a wife should be able to claim damages for enticement of her husband (58 per cent)
- a husband should be able to claim damages for enticement of his wife (52 per cent)

- a wife should be able to claim alimony from her husband (46 per cent)
- a man should be able to claim damages from a co-respondent for loss of his wife's services as housekeeper (46 per cent)

Finally, two in three felt that children in a marriage breaking up should be a reason against a divorce, and slightly more than one in two (54 per cent) thought that it was fair that the innocent party should always be given custody of any children.

In a political study conducted at the end of April, approval of the government had dropped to 40 per cent, with 48 per cent disapproving. Asked to name a new Conservative leader if anything happened to Winston Churchill, 70 per cent mentioned Anthony Eden. In the same study, the economy dominated the answers given to the question on which was the chief problem the government must solve in the next few months. Top of the list was the cost of living, mentioned by 27 per cent, followed by full employment (14 per cent), and other financial problems (11 per cent). When asked the degree to which they worried about various things, almost one in two said that they worried 'a lot' about making ends meet, while two in five worried to the same degree about getting proper food. Compared with February 1951, concern about making ends meet, food, old age, health, housing, and employment had risen, while concern about the possibility of another war had diminished.

The economy continued to dominate the early summer of 1952. In June, for example, the government and the trade unions were almost equally blamed for high prices, though world conditions and rearmament expenses were also given some responsibility. One in five of the public said that they were trying to cut down on 'everything', compared with only one in twenty-five the previous July. Top of the specific items people said that they were trying to cut down their spending on were smoking and cinemas. At the end of the month, four in five people thought that the country was facing a difficult economic situation, and two in three felt that they had been affected by a higher cost of living as a direct result of the Budget. On the other hand, by August, one in two thought that the government was doing all they could to meet the country's economic difficulties. One in three of the public felt otherwise. The public was similarly divided on the government's policy of discouraging wage claims as much as possible: with 55 per cent agreeing and 34 per cent disagreeing.

Of a more general nature were some of the other questions asked in the summer. 'Horror comics' were in vogue and two in three adults in Britain approved of an import ban on such comics. The public was more evenly divided, however, on the plan for television to be sponsored by advertisers, with roughly one third each approving, disapproving, or being undecided. Father, or the husband, was thought to have the main say in the family by a little under two in five people, while one in five said that the wife or mother did. The household chores people most liked doing were gardening or cooking, while washing-up, cleaning windows, attending to fires, and washing clothes were the least liked. On an abstract political concept, in Britain anyway, one in four said that they were aware of the Alternative Vote system. Those unaware were then given a brief explanation of what it meant and everyone was asked whether they approved or disapproved of this system of voting. Whereas two in five approved, almost as many, one in three, disapproved, with one in four unable to make up their minds. In October three in four adults thought it a good idea if every child in every country should have to learn another language besides their own, and one in two chose French as the second language.

In December the traditional year-end questions were asked as well as a few questions on two foreign problems - Kenya and Korea. Nine in ten of the public were aware of the troubles in Kenya, and among these they were evenly divided on their approval, or otherwise, of the way the government had been handling the problem. As far as Korea was concerned, the biggest proportion (43 per cent) wanted the United Nations to negotiate a peace while maintaining the battle lines. A little under one in five (17 per cent) thought the United Nations should pull out of Korea, while 18 per cent took a more hawkish line and wanted to continue with at least a 'limited war'. The stalemate in Korea is reflected in the public's general attitude towards the United Nations when asked in January 1953. Then 45 per cent felt that the United Nations had justified its existence, though 25 per cent thought otherwise. But satisfaction with the UN's progress was only 32 per cent, with 36 per cent expressing dissatisfaction. On a more soothing topic, what did the public like about 1952? The top three sporting personalities of the year were thought to be Randolph Turpin (boxer), Geoff Duke (motor-cyclist), and Len Hutton (cricketer). 'Educating Archie' was the favourite radio programme, followed by 'The Archers' and 'Take it From Here'. The top five films of the year were thought to be 'The Quiet Man', 'The Greatest Show on Earth', 'Mandy', 'The Sound Barrier', and 'Quo Vadis'. 'The Cruel Sea' topped the list of best books, followed by 'Kon Tiki Expedition', Churchill's memoirs, 'Struggle for Europe', and 'The Far Country'.

1953

In January Gallup asked people to look back to the war and to say whether there was much chance that the Nazis would again become powerful in Germany. One in three were uncertain and one in four thought that there was some chance, but most people, two in five, thought otherwise. One in three of those who thought that there was a chance felt that the best way to avoid it happening was to keep Germany under strict allied control. In the same survey questions were asked about Sunday Observance. The proportion, for example, approving of allowing theatres to open on Sundays stood at 50 per cent, with 41 per cent disapproving, but ten years earlier the proportion approving had stood at 58 per cent. On balance, by 48 per cent to 43 per cent, the public disapproved of professional sport on Sunday, and by more than two to one, 64 per cent to 26 per cent, disapproved of horse racing on the Sabbath.

In the run up to the Budget, the public's priorities on government expenditure were measured, with defence, family allowances, and food subsidies topping the list of things the public would cut down on first. On the other hand, the Health Service, housing and defence were top of the list of items to be cut down on last. When asked which taxes they would most like to reduce, a little over two in five chose purchase tax, while one in three chose income tax. The public were also almost evenly divided on the question of prices being allowed to go free while food rationing was disappearing. What would you do if you won £109,000 on the pools (although the figure would be much more these days)? One in four said that they would buy a home or make improvements to their current home, while one in five would spend the money on a holiday. When the Budget was announced, almost three in five (63 per cent) felt that it was a fair one and two in three saw Mr Butler doing a good job - the highest figure till then and since. The balance of opinion, however, was that it would not encourage people to work harder. The two things most liked about the Budget was the reduction in purchase tax on household articles and the reduction in income tax. The most unpopular item was the end of the excess profits tax. Approval of the government's record overall peaked at 60 per cent and has yet to be surpassed.

What did the public think about home cooking in 1953? An expert in food claimed that fewer than one in five women were really interested in preparing appetising food. Overall, 24 per cent of the public agreed with the expert - including 30 per cent of men and 19 per cent of women. One in five men said that they had a friend or relative (their mum?) in whose home they usually got better food than they did at home. The men were not particularly adventurous as far as food was concerned, with around three in five liking to try out something new at dinner. The proportion was even lower when a similar question was asked of married women: two in five said their husband liked something new being tried out on him, and fewer than one in three had done so in the past six months.

A number of questions on international affairs were asked in early summer, ranging across the invitation to the Japanese Crown Prince to attend the Coronation, Germany, Egypt and Korea. On the former, the public were fairly evenly balanced between whether it had been right or wrong to extend the invitation. Young people, the middle class and Conservatives supported the invitation, while senior citizens, the working class and Labour supporters were against. The public were also fairly evenly divided on whether to go ahead with the rearming of Germany, whatever happened, or to negotiate the question with Russia. In the dispute with Egypt, the public approved, by a margin of three to one, of the government's policy. In Korea, the peace negotiations were slowly drawing to a conclusion, though the British public had reservations about the way things were being handled. They disapproved, for example, of the offer of £35,000 being made to any pilot who would bring over a MIG fighter plane. They were more evenly balanced - with a little under one in three approving and slightly more disapproving - of the way the negotiations were being handled by the United Nations' representatives. Three in four felt that other nations should join in, rather than allowing the Americans to act as spokesmen for the United Nations in the negotiations. By a small margin, if there were to be an end to the fighting in Korea, people felt that China should be admitted as a member of the United Nations.

In May questions were asked about two very British institutions - the Health Service and cricket. Seven in ten of the public were satisfied with the treatment they got under the NHS, and the same proportion felt that they got value for money from the service. One in five said that they sometimes went outside the NHS for treatment: around one in twelve each going to a dentist, optician or doctor. One in three of the public claimed to take an interest in first class cricket, and the same proportion thought that England would win the Ashes. One in two opted for Australia winning. The outstanding batsmen of the series were thought to be Hutton and Miller, with Bedser, Trueman and Lindwall as the bowlers who would do well.

The Korean problem was returned to later in the year, with one in two in early August approving of the terms of the armistice. Almost as many, two in five, didn't know enough about the terms to answer the question.

The proportion of people who thought that there was much danger of world war was on the low side at 20 per cent. By December a similar proportion thought it likely that there would be further fighting in Korea. If the Communists did start fighting again, however, around two in five felt that Britain should continue to help the South Koreans, but one in three said no. A majority were actually against helping the South Koreans if they started fighting again, with fewer than one in five willing to help them. The public were more evenly divided on what the United Nations should do about the future of Korea: two in five felt an attempt should be made to unify the country, and slightly fewer opted for the status quo, with the North Koreans stopping at the truce line. There were also continuing problems in Africa. Nine in ten of the British public were aware of the Mau-Mau troubles in Kenya, and a little over two in five of these approved of the way the troubles were being handled. One in five disapproved, mainly because they felt the policies were too harsh.

'The Cruel Sea' was not only named as the best film people had seen in 1953, but it topped the list of best books read that year. Other popular films were 'Genevieve' and 'Quo Vadis' plus the films on the Coronation and on the conquest of Everest. The book of the latter event and the Kon Tiki Expedition completed the top three books for the year. 'Take It From Here' was the most popular radio programme of the year, followed by 'Have a Go' and 'Ray's a Laugh'. Gordon Pirie (runner) was voted sports personality of the year, with Stanley Matthews (footballer) as the runner-up and Len Hutton (cricketer) in third place.

1954

The year began with questions on the future of Prime Minister Churchill, with slightly more than one in two of the public thinking that he was too old (he was almost 80) for the job. A similar proportion felt that it would be a good thing for the country if he made way for a younger man, and one in two thought that he should be succeeded by Eden. In a later study, carried out at the end of February, Sir Winston topped the list of admired men, followed by the Duke of Edinburgh and Anthony Eden. The top three admired women were the Queen, Mrs Eleanor Roosevelt and the Queen Mother. As always, when asked, the public were not in favour of increasing MPs salaries, neither did they support the idea of MPs being entitled to pensions after ten years' service. When asked what was the salary for an MP, one in three did not know, but a little over one in two correctly put the annual figures as £10,000. On a related topic, that of the voting age, almost two in three were opposed to it being reduced to 18.

'Desert Island Discs'? No, desert island books! In February Gallup asked people which three books they would take with them if they were to be banished to a desert island. The most popular book by far, mentioned by a little over one in three people, was the Bible, followed by the works of Dickens, Shakespeare and encyclopedias. Nine in ten said that they had a Bible in their home, and two in three claimed to have read something in it since they left school. Other books to be found in the majority of homes were a cookery book (87 per cent), a dictionary (84 per cent) and a book on gardening (64 per cent).

In the same month questions were asked about the European Defence Community, an idea which was to finally fail later that year. Only one in three knew what EDC stood for, while another one in three had heard of it. One in two of this combined group thought that Britain should take a larger part in the Community, but around one in three thought otherwise. As far as the rearming of Germany was concerned, more people felt that the Western powers should be prepared to continue to negotiate on this point with the Russians. Given a choice, however, almost one in two wanted Germany to have an army which was part of a European army. In March three in five of the British public believed Russia's claim to have the H-bomb, and nine in ten were aware of the recent H-bomb test in the Pacific. Although three in four thought that a ban on the atom bomb was desirable, fewer than one in twenty thought that it was likely in the near future. One in four supported Russia's view that everyone should agree to ban all atom bombs, but more than twice as many sided with America in that we should have international inspection before trying to reach agreement. One in four of the public felt that the Russian H-bomb had made another war more likely, but twice as many thought it would have the opposite effect. The public, however, did not follow completely the American line on everything. Slightly more, for example, in late April disapproved of America's world role than approved. On the other hand, twelve times as many disapproved of Russia's role as approved. A little over one in two agreed with the view that Britain was giving in too much to the United States in her foreign policy, but one in three disagreed. One of our other war-time allies, France, was still having problems in the Far East, soon to be known as Vietnam. In fact they had just suffered a disastrous defeat at the hands of the Viet Minh at Dien Bien Phu. But three in four of the British public disapproved of sending troops to take part in the fighting, and almost two in three disapproved of sending air or naval forces to help the French.

On the same survey, something completely different! Three in four housewives said that they had tried the 'new margarine', and around one in three thought that it was as good as, or better than, butter, but slightly more thought that it was not as good. Naturally, given the difference in the price between the two products, the housewives said that they would be buying less butter in the future. Further questions about zebra crossings were asked in June. The crossings had proved so successful as far as the public was concerned that four in five wanted them to be kept, and seven in ten thought that they were not dangerous to use. It might seem incredible in this age of space travel that only one in four people had ever flown in a plane, and almost one in two of these had done so in the forces. When asked, almost one in two said that they would like to fly in a(nother) plane.

In September Gallup asked about the future of the two main party leaders. On the one hand, almost two in three of the public felt that Sir Winston Churchill should retire but, on the other hand, only one in four thought that Mr Attlee should do so. Eden was the preferred choice over Butler as Sir Winston's successor, while Morrison and Gaitskell were more popular than Bevan as Attlee's successor. At a local level, two in three claimed to know the name of their MP and a little under one in two of the public said that they had seen him or her at some time. Six per cent said that they had written to their MP and 13 per cent had talked to them.

1955

International affairs returned to the top of the pile of problems facing the government, as far as the public was concerned at the beginning of the year, with the cost of living dominating the list of problems facing the public themselves. Despite this latter finding, the public felt that on balance their standard of living was going up, though at the same time they were saying that they were finding it harder to make both ends meet than they had six months earlier. Further afield, the public were almost evenly divided on the question of Germany being given the right to have armed forces under NATO.

In what was going to be an election year, the Conservatives began with a slim one point lead over Labour, and a little over one in two of the public were satisfied with Churchill as Prime Minister and were satisfied with the government's performance to date. Two in three thought that Mr Butler was doing a good job as Chancellor of the Exchequer, and even more, four in five, thought that Sir Anthony Eden was doing a good job as Foreign Secretary. There was also majority approval (58 per cent) for the government's decision to make H-bombs and to be prepared to use them in the event of war between Russia and the West, though 31 per cent disapproved. Perhaps with recent United Nations' action over Korea in mind, one in two of the public opted to give control of Formosa to the UN, while around one in ten each felt that it should be left with Chiang Kai Shek or given to Communist China. In the event of an attack on Formosa from the mainland, the balance of opinion was that we should join with America to resist the attack, though the largest group of people were undecided on this question. Despite the potential problem over Formosa, three in five of the British public felt that Communist China should be admitted to the United Nations. The replies were less clear cut on whether Chiang Kai Shek should be allowed to remain as a member: two in five thought he should but one in four felt otherwise.

That health scourge of Britain, the common cold, was prevalent in the winter of 1954/55, with seven in ten of the public succumbing to one by late February. The main thing done to try to rid themselves of it was to take an analgesic, the choice of one in three sufferers, while around one in four took a hot drink, usually with a slug of alcohol in it. A little under one in five sufferers did nothing to try to ease the symptoms. Despite the high incidence of colds, most people rated their general state of health as good or very good. One in five thought that it was fair, while four per cent thought it was poor. Fewer than one in two people had been to a doctor in the last six months, though one in three had bought medicines from a chemist rather than bother about going to see their doctor. Gallup were also asking questions about that other seemingly British winter problem - drink and driving. Three in four of the public felt that it would be a good thing if motorists involved in a serious accident were to be automatically tested for their blood alcohol level, and three in four also felt that such drivers should have to pass another driving test before they were allowed to drive again. Around three in five felt that the driving test should be repeated every few years in any case, and four in five thought that cars should be tested every year for roadworthiness.

The Royal Family were in the news again, concerning the relationship between Princess Margaret and the divorcee, Group Captain Townsend. Nine in ten of the public had heard of the discussions regarding a marriage, and two in three of these felt that Captain Townsend being divorced should not be a reason why Princess Margaret should not marry him. The public were more evenly divided over the press coverage of such events: around one in two thought that newspapers should write about these things, particularly if done properly, but almost as many thought they should not. Gallup returned to the topic later in the year and three in five said that they would approve if Princess Margaret and Captain Townsend wanted to marry. The main reason given by the minority disapproving was the fact of the divorce. Not surprisingly, three in five of the public overall disagreed with the ruling of the Archbishop of Canterbury that the Church of England should not marry a divorced person so long as the other party was still alive.

By April the Conservatives' lead over Labour had widened slightly to four per cent, and the public's initial reaction to Prime Minister Eden was a handsome 73 per cent vote of approval. The public were less certain, however, on whether he should call an election or wait, though the balance of opinion was for an early election. When asked who would win the election, one in two thought that it would be the Conservatives, while one in five thought that Labour would emerge victorious. The Conservatives were returned with an increased majority. One in four, after the event, thought that prosperity had been the main reason for the Conservative victory, followed by the differing unity of the two main parties: the Conservatives united, Labour divided. It is perhaps a sad reflection on the British media that many stories appearing in newspapers during the summer need to be excused due to the 'silly season'. Some of the questions asked in the summer of 1955 also have that slight air of eccentricity, but there is no doubt that they were designed with serious intentions in mind. Three in five of the public, for example, disapproved of the Home Secretary's decision to make it allowable to take the eggs of 13 common birds. The public, however, were much more evenly divided on the link between atomic explosions and the relatively poor weather of recent years: two in five thought that there was a link and the same proportion discounted it.

In a special autumn Budget Mr Butler raised both purchase tax and distributed profits tax, as well as imposing a credit squeeze. His rating as Chancellor, which had stood at 57 per cent in April before the election and with a generous spring Budget, fell to 52 per cent in September and to 43 per cent in October. The Prime Minister's rating, too, was hit and it was down to 63 per cent in October, though this was still a high level. On the other hand, one in two felt that Mr Butler had been right to impose a credit squeeze and a little over one in five thought that they had been affected by it.

As the Korean war declined in peoples' memories, the public became less critical of the United Nations. Three in five, for example, thought that it had justified its existence during its first ten years, and two in five felt that ordinary people could influence government policy so far as it involved the UN. One in three, however, saw ordinary people as being impotent in this respect. The idea of a United Nations' force made up of men from all countries was received with mixed feelings, perhaps scepticism, by the British people. Slightly under two in five supported the idea, but two in five were against it. Nevertheless, if the force were to be set up, around three in five thought that Britain should supply men to be part of it. Even more, two in three, thought that Britain should help if another country were attacked and the United Nations called for help, and the majority of these felt that we should help regardless of the kind of government the attacked country might have. If a war came, would the public sanction the use of the H- bomb? Not in October 1955 if the enemy did not have an H-bomb themselves. Three quarters disapproved of its use in this situation, and two in three disapproved of using it against an enemy that had it but was not using it. Against an enemy, however, who had the weapon and was using it against Britain, naturally, three in four approved of its use. On a more peaceful level, people were asked their attitudes to Britain's aid to the developing countries. A little over one in two felt that Britain was doing enough to help the 'countries with a lower standard of living than our own' and one in five thought that we were actually doing too much, but around one in seven thought we should do more.

Back in July, immediately after the execution of Ruth Ellis for murder, one in two had agreed that most people convicted of murder should be sentenced to death, but a little over one in three wanted the death penalty abolished. Four in five supporting the death penalty said it should be imposed regardless of sex. When the questions were repeated in late November, support for the death penalty had risen 11 points to 61 per cent, while the proportion of abolitionists had declined by 12 points to 25 per cent. The vast majority of people wanting the retention of capital punishment still wanted it imposed on women. In February 1956 a slightly different question was asked, dividing people into three groups:

- keep death penalty as it is (30 per cent)
- keep death penalty for worst cases (39 per cent)
- abandon the death penalty (21 per cent)

When asked whether they would approve or disapprove if Parliament were to remove the death penalty for an experimental period of five years, 45 per cent approved of the idea, while 41 per cent disapproved. As a presage of things to come, it is easy with hindsight to look at two questions Gallup asked towards the end of 1955. The first of these dealt with the supply of arms to Egypt by Russia and what the West's reaction to this should be. One in three, the second biggest answer, said 'don't know', but slightly more, two in five, thought that the Western powers should supply the United Nations' Commission with arms. One in ten felt that Israel should be supplied with arms, while one in seven said 'do nothing'. The second question asked what was Russia's object and the public were evenly divided in their answers, with one third each seeing it as Russia making certain of her security, or as imperialist aggression, or were undecided. Then in January it was discovered that government military surplus stocks had been exported to Belgium and re-exported to Egypt. Given the above results, almost three in five of the public disapproved of the government's handling of the affair, with a little over one in ten supporting them.

When it came to the traditional year-end questions, two 'Doctor' films were among the most popular. Top film of 1955 was thought to be 'The Dam Busters', followed by 'Doctor at Sea', 'Doctor in the House' and 'The Robe'. The top five most popular radio programmes were 'Have a Go', 'The Archers', 'Take It From Here', 'The Goon Show' and 'Life With the Lyons'. Wilfred Pickles, host of the top radio programme, was also involved in one of the most popular television programmes. Top place went to 'What's My Line?' with 'Ask Pickles' in second place. Jockeying for third place were three programmes: 'Sports View', 'Sports Special' and the 'Dave King Show'. The most popular book of the year had also appeared in earlier years - 'The Cruel Sea' by Nicholas Monsarrat. The runners-up were two other war books, 'Reach For The Sky', and 'HMS Ulysses'. Gordon Pirie (runner) was voted outstanding sports personality of the year, followed by Chris Chataway (another athlete), Stanley Matthews (footballer) and Pat Smythe (showjumper).

1956

In the middle of January Gallup had the foresight to ask a question based on one of those pronouncements which have a habit of returning to haunt their authors. The Astronomer Royal had been quoted as saying that the prospects of being able to travel in space, outside the earth, was 'utter bilge' and a little over one in three agreed with him. But one in three, brought up on the likes of Flash Gordon, disagreed and another third couldn't make up their minds either way. Closer to home, international affairs, as in 1955, were thought to be the most urgent problem facing the government. One in three mentioned such problems as Cyprus and the Middle East, while one in four thought that the cost of living was the most urgent problem. Satisfaction with Eden started out at 50 per cent in February, dropped to 45 per cent a month later, and further still to 41 per cent by April. Approval of the government's record overall, too, had fallen from 44 per cent in December to 34 per cent in March. Similarly, only one in three approved of the way the government was handling the Cyprus problem, with as many disapproving. Mr Macmillan, the new Chancellor of the

Exchequer, was also poorly rated, with almost twice as many people thinking he was doing a bad job as thought he was doing well.

A little over thirty years ago, Gallup asked about the ubiquitous parking meter. Two in five of the general public agreed with the suggestion that they should be installed for all street parking in big cities, but one in four disagreed. A proposal that the speed limit in some built-up areas should be raised from 30 mph to 40 mph was decisively rejected by two in three people, with only one in five supporting the idea. In the same survey, questions were asked about the diseases people were most concerned with. Cancer topped the list with 14 per cent of diseases or complaints people thought about, followed by tuberculosis (6 per cent). Naturally, when asked which complaint killed most people in Britain, these two diseases were in the top three given. Cancer (41 per cent) was again top of the list, with heart troubles (14 per cent) in second place and tuberculosis (13 per cent) a close third. Even more morbidly, were two questions asked in May about cremations. Two in three adults approved of cremations, and a quarter disapproved. A similar split emerged when people were asked what their wish would be for themselves when they died: one in two chose to be cremated, while one in three opted for burial.

Althought Mr Macmillan's spring Budget was not particularly well received - two in five thinking it fair, but two in five thinking it unfair - his personal rating as Chancellor improved markedly compared with a month earlier. Now more thought he was doing a good job than saw him doing badly. His proposal for a state lottery was approved of by a little over one in two of the public, though one in three disapproved - particularly people at the bottom end of the social scale. The public were initially less enthusiastic about buying the new premium bonds, however, with slightly more than one in four interested in buying them and another one in five who thought they might buy them.

While Hugh Gaitskell had been elected leader of the Labour party in December 1955 after Attlee's retirement, it was not until May that the public was asked to rate the new leader. Then, 42 per cent thought that he was a good leader, while 24 per cent thought otherwise. At the same time, the public's rating of Prime Minister Eden had improved to 54 per cent being satisfied with him, though Labour was 4 points ahead of the Conservatives in voting intentions.

In early summer Gallup conducted two related studies: on lung cancer in May, followed by a major survey of attitudes towards the National Health Service. The first of these was based around a statement by the Minister of Health and the degree to which people were aware of what he had said. Altogether four in five said that they had read or heard of the statement and most of these thought that he had suggested a link between smoking and lung cancer. Seven in ten people felt that the question was important and one in four said that they or someone they knew was intending to cut down on their smoking or stop altogether. The second survey consisted of a sample of both general practitioners and of the general public. Among the general practitioners, two in three said that if they had a chance to go back ten years and vote on whether the National Health Service should be started, they would have voted in favour of it but one in three said they would have voted against it. A majority of the GPs said that they had noticed that patients were asking for more medicines and appliances than before the NHS started, while two in five said that patients were asking for more certificates than before and one in three were asking for more home visits. One in three felt that their relationships with patients had become more impersonal and slightly more, two in five, said that they sometimes had difficulty in getting their patients into hospital without delay. In terms of the financial side of the NHS, three in four were opposed to a full-time salaried service and three in four favoured partnerships. A little over one in two favoured the idea of group practices, while two in five favoured Health Centres. Finally, the average number of patients on a list to be able to treat them properly was thought to be around 2600, for which they expected an income of around £3000.

The patients' reaction to the National Health Service was very positive and complimentary: nine in ten, for example, giving it a positive score on a rating scale to produce an average score of +63 on a scale running from -100 to +100. Nine in ten also felt that they received a good service from the NHS, eight in ten thought that their doctor gave them enough of his time, and eight in ten felt that the doctor did not mind being asked to visit them at home. In fact, a little over one in three had asked their doctor for a night visit and the bulk of these thought the doctor did not seem to mind. Eight in ten saw their doctor as a friend in whom they could confide. The biggest complaint came on having to pay one shilling (5p) for a prescription, and though 64 per cent thought this was fair, 29 per cent thought it otherwise.

The nationalisation of the Suez Canal was announced on 27 July and a week later Gallup conducted the first of a number of studies on what was to be the major event of the period. Not surprisingly, the British public took a hostile view of Egypt's actions, with two in three thinking that they were not acting within their rights, two in three thinking that they could not be trusted to keep the canal open to all shipping and three in five felt that the Egyptians would not be able to run the canal with reasonable efficiency. Majorities approved of the main British and French moves, though the public were evenly divided on whether or not Egypt should be allowed to keep the canal some time in the future. Only one in three of the public opted for military action if Egypt did not accept the decisions of the international conference, with a little under one in two preferring economic and political action. Only one in four approved of the idea of supplying arms to Israel, with more than twice as many disapproving. A fortnight later around three in five said that they approved of the way the government had handled the situation, but this proportion fell to two in five by mid-September. Two in three felt that Britain and France were right in not taking military action against Egypt immediately when Nasser seized the Suez Canal and a similar proportion wanted to refer the matter to the United Nations if Egypt deliberately interferred with the free passage of shipping in the canal. Fewer than one in five, however, felt that Sir Anthony Eden would have to resign over Suez and almost three in five of the public were satisfied with him as Prime Minister. Approval of the military action increased from 37 per cent in early November to 49 per cent a month later, with one in three thinking that Britain and France should have continued the action until they had occupied the whole of the Suez Canal zone. On 19 November Eden's illness had been announced and he retired with 56 per cent of the public still satisfied with him. He was succeeded by Harold Macmillan, the public's second choice behind Butler.

In the world of entertainment, the public voted Flora Robson as best actress of the year and Peter Cushing the best actor. 'Sunday Night at the Palladium', still on the small screen, was voted best regular television programme, Peter Haigh was voted as the best commentator, Eamonn Andrews the best variety artist and Lady Isobel Barnett the best female personality.

4 1957-1964 : The Macmillan Administration

The public's initial reaction to Harold Macmillan was positive, with one in two approving of his appointment as prime minister, and the balance of opinion thinking that Mr Butler would have been a worse choice. One in two also felt that the government should carry on, though two in five thought that there should be a general election. When asked what was the most urgent problem facing the government, Suez topped the list with 38 per cent, followed by the cost of living (20 per cent). The balance of opinion was that the change in leadership would help to settle the Suez question, but the public were evenly divided on whether it would bring peace to the Middle East. The change was expected to help improve Commonwealth relations and improve relations with the United States, but, closer to home, it was not thought to stop the bitter political arguments of the previous months.

In February, as part of a major study into religion in Britain, people were asked what they had done on the previous Sunday. One in seven said that they had gone to church, compared to almost two in three who had listened to the radio and the one in two who had watched television. A little over one in four said that they went to a place of worship at least once a month, and the same proportion said they regularly listened to religious services on radio or watched them on television. Three in four claimed to have gone to Sunday school as a child. As far as beliefs were concerned, two in five believed in a personal god and slightly fewer thought that there was some sort of spirit, god or life force. Seven in ten believed that Jesus Christ was the son of God, though only one in three felt that there was a devil. Similarly, while one in two believed in life after death, one in two thought that it was not possible to exchange messages with the dead. Almost everyone believed in teaching children to say their prayers, but only three in five thought that they should go to Sunday school (if they wanted to). In the same month, 41 per cent of the public said they would emigrate if they could - the highest figure since 1948.

Despite rising living standards, 1957 was to be a year of strikes and unemployment. In March, therefore, Gallup conducted two separate surveys on strikes, the first being a nationwide study where people were asked to say who was to blame for the strikes. One in three blamed the workers, one in four blamed the employers and one in four thought that both groups were equally at fault. At the same time, a sample of strikers and their wives was interviewed in the affected dockyard areas. Naturally, the results told a different story than that told by the national sample. More than four in five thought that the employers had been wrong to refuse to offer any pay increase and seven in ten felt that the unions had been right to call the strike. Three in four strikers thought that something worthwhile would be achieved by the strike, though their wives were less sure, and two in three disapproved of the government's handling of the situation. Even among the general public as a whole, the balance of opinion was marginally in the government's favour. Mr Thorneycroft's Budget was not particularly well received, with almost as many saying it was not fair as thought it was a fair one, though his personal rating as Chancellor was slightly better. Overall, 42 per cent saw the Budget as being fair and 50 per cent felt he was doing a good job as Chancellor. A little over one in two (53 per cent) thought that the Budget would not help them at all, while 34 per cent felt it might be a little help.

The year 1957 saw the successful testing of Britain's hydrogen bomb, though the public was decidedly less than enthusiastic about the event. In a survey in early April, for example, a little over one in two (54 per cent) agreed with the scientists who were saying that the tests were a serious threat to public health and to the health of future generations. Only one in five felt that the fears were not well-founded. The public were almost evenly divided on the decision to carry out the tests: 41 per cent approving and 44 per cent disapproving. In a similar study a month later, agreement with the fearful scientists had increased, though approval of the tests had also risen, possibly due to a feeling of a fait accompli. Around one in eight said that they were worried a lot about the talk of hydrogen bombs, rockets and guided missiles, one third were worried a little but one in two were not worried at all. At the end of the month, one in two approved of the idea of stopping further tests regardless of what other countries did, while another one in three said that they would agree, rather unrealistically, if all other nations agreed to stop testing nuclear weapons.

Writing in the age of the motor car and 'motorway madness', it is perhaps worthwhile to look back thirty years to when only one in five drove a car - less than a third of the level in the United States at the same time. One in four motorists had been involved in a car accident, compared with one in three American motorists, and the British motorist was also less likely to have been stopped for speeding than their American counterparts, 13 per cent and 18 per cent respectively. The average weekly mileage, however, and despite the disparity in the nations' sizes, was slightly higher in Britain than in the wide open spaces across the Atlantic.

And just to show that male chauvinism is nothing new, more than one in two male motorists felt that men were the better drivers, though one in five female motorists shared this view.

In August a detailed study was conducted on how the public spent their leisure time. Almost nine in ten, for example, said they had listened to the radio over the previous seven days, compared with two in three watching television. The most popular hobbies or leisure time activities, apart from sports, were knitting, gardening, needlework and reading. A little over one in ten said that they were taking evening classes, a correspondence course or were doing studies in their spare time. More than one in two (55 per cent) were reading a magazine, while half as many were reading a book. Perhaps surprisingly, a little over one in four said they were sometimes at a loss what to do, though two in five said they would like to have more spare time. Two in three housewives felt that the other members of the family did as much as she thought they should to help her, but one in four thought they could do with more help. On average, housewives in 1957 went out shopping three days in the week, and around one in two managed to get a 'day off' at least once a week. On a more general topic, one in two of the public said that they felt tired most of the time, though nine in ten thought that their health was at least fair.

In the wider sphere of international relations, questions were asked about Britain's membership of the Common Market. On all questions the 'don't knows' were the largest group, amounting to almost one in two of the public. This aside, the public, by a margin of two to one, thought that Britain should join the Common Market. The public were also undecided about the so-called 'Eisenhower Doctrine' (the policy America was pursuing in the Middle East). Though among those people with an opinion, those approving equalled those disapproving. The public's view of Russia's involvement in the Middle East was decidedly more certain, with three in five thinking that Russia was more interested in stirring up trouble there than in promoting peace.

In September support for Labour reached the fifties in percentage terms for the fourth time in the year, peaking at 52 per cent, their second highest level of support since the war. Hugh Gaitskell as party leader, however, was less popular than his party and less popular than Harold Macmillan. Labour's advantage was probably a reaction to the increase in the Bank Rate in mid-September, and they became at the same time the public's choice as the probable winners of the next election, whenever it might come. In comparison to the beginning of the year when the most urgent problem facing the government was thought to be the international situation, by September the economic situation dominated the replies.The public's preoccupation with the economy is mirrored in the replies to other questons asked at that time. Around two in three, for example, felt that prices would go up yet the same proportion thought that it would be more difficult to get wage increases and almost one in two felt that unemployment would rise. By November the balance of opinion was that Mr Thorneycroft was doing a bad job as Chancellor.

In the same month Gallup published reactions to the Wolfenden Committee about the law on prostitution and homosexuality. A little over one in three accepted that homosexual behaviour between men aged 21 and over should not be a criminal act provided that it was carried out in private (38 per cent), and that the 'call girl' system had to be allowed to go on and should not be made illegal (35 per cent). A little under one in two, 47 per cent and 46 per cent respectively, disagreed with these recommendations. Fifty-six per cent regarded prostitution as a more serious problem than homosexuality, 42 per cent thought homosexuality more serious. Among men, 47 per cent said that they had at some time been accosted by a prosititute in the street, and 19 per cent had been approached by a homosexual.

As the year came to a close, people were asked what had been the outstanding world event of 1957. Top of the list was the 'Sputnik', followed by the Queen's tour, while their holiday was the event which stood out most on a personal basis. The best film of the year was thought to be the musical 'The King and I', with Tolstoy's 'War and Peace' in second place and 'The Battle of the River Plate' third. BBC's 'Panorama' topped the list of favourite television programmes, followed by 'The Palladium Show' and 'What's My Line?'. The top three radio programmes were 'The Archers', 'The Goon Show' and 'Have a Go'. The outstanding sports personality of 1957 was thought to be the athlete Derek Ibbotson, with Stirling Moss and Donald Campbell taking the next two places. Two in five felt that the most urgent problem facing themselves or their family in 1958 would be the cost of living, while one in two mentioned the economy as the biggest problem facing the government. One in three thought that foreign affairs would be the government's main problem and one in seven felt that it would be the question of defence.

Russia was, on balance, thought to be winning the 'Cold War', though a majority felt that the West could continue to live more or less peacefully with the Russians. Two in three of the public disapproved of allowing ballistic missile sites to be set up in Britain if some of them were under American control, but they were almost evenly divided on the sites if they were all under British control.

1958

Russian peace moves were treated with typical British conservatism: one in three were hopeful about them, one in three were hopeful but suspicious, and around one in five simply suspicious. When asked about top level talks between the West and Russia - which three in four wanted - almost one in two thought that they had little chance of being successful, while a hopeful one third gave them much chance of success. Russian leader Bulganin's note - suggesting top level talks, a ban on atomic tests and atomic weapons, troop reductions, inspection zones and an expansion of East-West trade - was well- received by the British public, with majorities ranging from three in five to over three in four thinking the West should agree to the individual proposals. One in four also felt that Russia was justified in refusing to participate in the United Nations Disarmament Commission on the ground that only 3 out of the 25 members of the Commission were communist countries, though almost twice as many felt that the objection was not justified. On balance, the public's view was that both the British Government's reaction and America's had been too cautious.

January started badly on the domestic front for Mr Macmillan, with his sacking of monetarist Chancellor Thorneycroft. By a margin of two to one the public sided with the deposed Chancellor rather than with the Prime Minister. Even Conservatives were evenly divided in their support for the two personalities. The affair, however, had little effect on voting intentions, though Mr Macmillan's personal rating fell 11 points. One rather marked longer-term shift was in the public's perception of the parties as a whole. In April 1955 three in four thought that there were important differences between the parties, but by January 1958 the proportion had dropped to only two in five, with more actually seeing the parties as all much of a muchness. Support for the Liberals at this time rose to 19 per cent, their highest level of national support then in Gallup's files, with one in three saying they would consider voting for them if they thought the party would get a majority in a general election. In March the Liberals captured Torrington, their first by-election gain in 30 years (though they were to have no other such successes that year and their national support declined).

In the social sphere, questions were asked in March about artificial insemination, known to some degree by nine in ten of the public. One in two disapproved of the idea where the donor was unknown to both partners, and the public was almost evenly divided on its legality, even when both parties agreed. Where a wife could not have children by her own husband and resorted to AID without her husband's consent, a majority felt that this should be grounds for divorce. On a general question on divorce, 36 per cent opted for the status quo, 10 per cent thought that divorce should be made easier, 28 per cent said make it more difficult and 11 per cent were completely against divorce, including one in two Catholics.

Mr Thorneycroft's replacement as Chancellor of the Exchequer, Mr Heathcoat Amory, received the equivalent of a standing ovation from the public in their reaction to his first Budget: 62 per cent thinking it was fair - the highest figure then recorded for a Budget - though two in five expressed some disappointment with it. While the Budget had no immediate impact on the levels of party support, the proportion of the public who gave a positive rating to the idea of voting for the Conservatives at the next election rose from 41 per cent in October 1957 to 51 per cent in April.

With an increasing feeling of deja vu, this writer returns to questions in May 1958 on the British Sunday. By then, television (51 per cent) had overtaken radio (47 per cent) as the main Sunday activity, with only 12 per cent saying that they went to church. A majority (56 per cent) of the public felt that the government should agree to set up a Royal Commission to enquire into the laws affecting Sunday. On possible changes in the law, the public were more evenly divided: greatest approval (50 per cent), for example, was for places of entertainment being allowed to open on Sundays as on weekdays but almost as many (39 per cent) disapproved. Similarly, slightly more (46 per cent) approved of the idea of professional sport on the Sabbath, with 41 per cent disapproving. The balance of opinion was reversed, however, 39 per cent and 44 per cent respectively, on allowing public houses to open the same hours on Sunday as during the week. Overall, slightly more (47 per cent) felt that Sunday should be like any other day of the week as far as the law was concerned, rather than it should be subject to special legal restrictions (41 per cent). Two in three churchgoers, however, were in favour of such restrictions. On a completely different topic, though an equally recurring one, a little over one in three of the public felt that cigarette smoking was one of the causes of lung cancer, with a little under one in three disagreeing.

In the world of women's fashion, the 'trapeze line' was investigated in June 1958. One in three men and two in three women said they were aware of what the 'trapeze line' looked like, and around one half of these said that they disliked it. Only among young women was there a balance of opinion in favour of the new fashion, and, naturally, it was mainly among this group that wearers of it would be found.

By late June the Conservatives were just 3.5 per cent behind Labour and the public's rating of both Mr Macmillan and his government showed

significant increases over previous months. At the same time, problems
arose yet again in the Middle East, and a majority of the British public
approved of the idea of sending British and American troops to Lebanon
if the United Nations were to do so, but, with perhaps Suez in mind, a
majority disapproved of such an action without being sanctioned by the
United Nations. In mid-July majorities approved of America sending troops
to Lebanon (52 per cent) and of British troops being sent to Jordan (54
per cent). Labour's line on the crisis was disapproved of by a margin of
three to two.

The summer of 1958 was also marked by racial disturbances in
Nottingham and in Notting Hill, London. In June, for example, the owner
of a dance hall in Wolverhampton had refused to admit coloured men to
dances there, a policy disapproved of by a margin of almost three to one
of the public. In September further quesions were asked of a more general
nature on attitudes towards coloured immigrants from the Commonwealth.
Altogether, 55 per cent wanted restrictions on coloured immigrants but
almost as many (49 per cent) wanted restrictions applied to whites. One
in three said that they would consider moving if coloured people came to
live next door, rising to three in five if the coloured people were in great
numbers. The public were in favour, on balance, of allowing coloured
people from the Commonwealth to compete for jobs in Britain on equal
terms with people born here but were against a similar freedom so far as
council house waiting lists were concerned. Only 7 per cent said that they
would object if there were coloured children in the same class at school
as their own children, but 71 per cent said that they disapproved of mixed
marriages.

As the year came to a close, support for the Liberals declined to around
only one in ten, while support for the Conservatives increased, putting
them 4 points ahead of Labour. Mr Macmillan, too, was more popular
after the doldrums of the spring, and he enjoyed a personal advantage in
excess of 10 points over Mr Gaitskell. By December one in two said that
they approved of the government's record to date, its highest level since
the 1955 General Election.

According to the public, the outstanding events of 1958 were satellites,
sputniks and rockets; the Pope's death and the election of a new Pope;
Nautilus's voyage under the North Pole; and the troubles in Cyprus.
European swimming champion Ian Black and world champion racing driver
Mike Hawthorn tied for first place as sports personality of the year, followed
by cricketer Peter May, racing driver Stirling Moss, swimmer Judy Grinham
and Donald Campbell, fastest man on water. 'The Bridge on the River
Kwai' was voted film of the year, with 'The Ten Commandments', 'South

Pacific' and 'Around the World in 80 Days' runners-up. On the small screen, the two most popular programmes were 'Panorama' and 'Tonight', while the top two radio programmes of 1957, 'The Archers' and 'The Goon Show' again took the honours.

1959

The election year opened with the Conservatives ahead by the narrowest of margins - one half of one per cent - and with unemployment thought to be the most urgent problem facing the government. The public's rating of Mr Gaitskell had tended to improve through the winter and he went from 13 points behind Mr Macmillan in November to 6 points behind in January. The public were, on balance, in favour of the way the government was handling the economy and social services, but disapproved of their policies on employment and on foreign affairs. Majorities also felt that the government was spending enough on defence, space travel and on education, but not enough on pensions or on roads. It was not surprising, therefore, that the public put highest priority on increasing pensions, putting increased expenditure on defence and space at the bottom.

Equally of little surprise, three in four of the British public were not prepared to pay more taxes towards space travel and around two in five felt that Britain should do nothing about it. By a margin of nine to one Russia was thought to be ahead in the field of long range missiles and rockets, and more credit was given to former German scientists for both America's and Russia's progress in the field than was given to their own scientists. Around one in three felt that God had not meant us to go in for such things and also felt that we ran the risk of affecting the earth by upsetting the balance of the planets. Fewer than one in ten - including one in four young adults - expressed any interest in being the first person to go up in an earth satellite, though one in two felt that they were fortunate to be living in an age when space developments were going ahead at such a pace.

That the parties were gearing up to an election can be seen by their respective degrees of activity early in the year. In mid-February, for example, 8 per cent had been called on by the Conservative party in the previous three months. Five per cent recalled a visit from Labour, while almost nobody recalled a visit by a Liberal. Similarly, 27 per cent recalled advertising for the Conservatives, as against 15 per cent for Labour and only 3 per cent for the Liberals. Full employment, followed by inflation, were thought to be the important issues of the election in influencing which way people might vote. Mr Macmillan's Moscow visit was well received, with seven in ten before the event favouring top-level talks between the West and Russia, and eight in ten approving of the trip itself. After the event, a similar proportion felt that Mr Macmillan had been right to make the trip and people thought that it had achieved something. The trip also increased the proportion thinking that Russia, America and Britain wanted to end the Cold War. Three in five of the public said that they would accept, if offered, a fortnight's all-expenses paid trip to Russia.

Heathcoat Amory's second Budget proved almost as popular as his first, and only Mr Butler in 1953 achieved a higher personal rating as Chancellor. At the same time, disputes arose between Russia and the West over the future of Berlin. One in two of the public either felt that an agreement would be reached with both sides giving something away or that they would just continue arguing. Only 2 per cent thought that it would lead to a war, though one in three felt that Russia and the West would go to war over Berlin. If war were to break out over Berlin, one in four thought that it would be a conventional war but one in three thought that nuclear weapons would be used. Despite the risk of a war, people felt that the allied forces should be kept in Berlin, and one in two thought the East German Government should be recognised if the Russians handed over their sector of Berlin to them.

The impact of foreign affairs on domestic politics can be seen in the personal ratings of Mr Macmillan and Mr Gaitskell. While the former's increased to more than 60 per cent, Mr Gaitskell's stuck in the mid-forties. Approval of the government's handling of foreign affairs was second only to their handling of the economy. In July people were asked whether they would like to see a number of specific policies in their party's election programmes and there was over-whelming support for a ban on nuclear weapons and for an East-West summit meeting. Three in four also wanted more spent on improving roads and almost two in three wanted to reduce prescription charges. On the other hand, people were almost evenly divided on the question of discontinuing with the eleven-plus examination, while the idea of unilateral disarmament was rejected by a margin of almost two to one. Even among Labour supporters, a majority opposed unilateralism.

The Conservatives began the election with a slim advantage over Labour both in party support and in terms of who was expected to win the election (the latter usually a good indicator of what would happen). When asked what would be the most important issues discussed at the election, the top three issues mentioned were nuclear weapons, pensions and the cost of living - two issues favourable to the Conservatives and one for Labour. The gap narrowed between the two parties at the end of September and it appeared that Labour might actually win the election, though the

Conservatives were still the party expected to win. On the day, the Conservatives won by a little over 4 per cent and gained a majority of almost 100 seats over Labour.

One of the early policies introduced by the new government was the Betting and Gaming Bill in November. Eight in ten of the public, given the Bill's subject, were aware of it and three in five approved of allowing bookmakers to open betting shops for off-course betting. Altogether, around one in three of the public felt that they might use the new outlets, given the opportunity. The public was less enamoured, however, about legalising roulette, dice or other games of chance, though, even so, a little under one in two approved of the idea, while one in three disapproved. On the question of opening licensed gaming casinos, the public were evenly divided: with two in five each in favour or opposed. This was at a time when almost one in two of the adult population did the pools and altogether three in four lived in a household where someone did them.

In December 1959 and January 1960 Gallup organisations in 13 countries, covering parts of Europe, the Americas and Asia, combined to conduct a survey on the general theme of the sixties. For the British, Winston Churchill and the Duke of Edinburgh had been the two outstanding personalities of the previous decade, while Russia and Britain were thought to be the countries who could look back with most satisfaction for what they had achieved during the 1950s. Looking ahead 10 years, the British took an optimistic view of the future, with one in two thinking that the world would be a better place to live in. Only one in ten thought that it would not be so good. The USA, followed by Britain, were the countries the British thought would have the highest standard of living in 10 years' time, while Russia was thought to be heading for the top position in the field of science and towards having the strongest military forces. With an extra touch of patriotism, two in three Britons thought that Britain would be the country with the most to offer ordinary people for happiness and contentment. When asked to look 20 years ahead, to 1980, and to say whether a number of things would have happened by then, the predictions were:

-    a cure for cancer will have been found (65 per cent)
-    man will have landed on the Moon (61 per cent)
-    Russia and the West will be living peacefully together (41 per cent)
-    our standard of living will have doubled (40 per cent)
-    expectation of life will have risen to 100 years (33 per cent)

- all countries will have ceased to manufacture H-bombs or anything like them (32 per cent)
- we will be able to travel anywhere in the world without a passport (30 per cent)
- we will be working a three-day week (13 per cent)
- Russian communism will have vanished (12 per cent)
- atomic war between Russia and America (6 per cent)
- capitalism and the Western way of life will have collapsed (6 per cent)
- civilisation as we know it will be in ruins (4 per cent)

Internationally, the British appeared optimistic in this survey, with two in three thinking that it was possible to reach a peaceful settlement of differences between Russia and the West, and three in five thinking that there was not much danger of war. Similarly, a little under two in three felt that it was very important that we tried to make a success of the United Nations but only one in three thought that it was doing a good job. They also felt that both the British and the human race were getting better from the viewpoint of both health and intelligence, but getting worse in terms of honesty. The vast majority (84 per cent) of people had a Bible in their home, 80 per cent had a cookery book, 75 per cent had a dictionary and 28 per cent claimed to have a book of Shakespeare's plays. Around one in four Britons said that they had read something in the Bible in the previous seven days, while almost twice as many said that it was longer than a year ago or could not remember when.

The best film of the year was thought to be 'South Pacific', followed by the Biblical epic, 'The Ten Commandments', and 'The Bridge on the River Kwai' - almost a repeat of the 1958 popularity stakes. By a wide margin, the most urgent problem facing people in 1960 was thought to be the cost of living, mentioned by more than two in five of the public.

1960

There was little change in the standing of the three main parties in the three months after the general election: the Conservatives beginning 1960 with a 3.5 per cent lead over Labour with support for the Liberals below 10 per cent. In the week leading up to Christmas 1959, Gallup began a regular series of political ratings, then christened the Gallup Political Index, but long since discontinued and now only remembered through the title of Gallup's monthly publication of political, social and economic data. The first few months showed defence, international affairs and the economy battling each other as the most important problems facing the country and the goverment scored higher than the opposition on all these issues. Only on the question of housing, labour relations and pensions did the opposition do better than the government.

In line with the study on the Betting and Gaming Bill in late 1959, February saw the publication of another study of a British institution, 'The Declining Football Audience'. A little over one in four men, for example, claimed to have gone to watch professional soccer in the previous four weeks, and a little over one in ten had watched amateur soccer. Comparing the end of the fifties with the beginning of the decade, attendances at Football League matches in the season had declined by almost seven million. What had turned the crowds away? The main reason given for not going was that they no longer liked the game, mentioned by around one in three, followed by having to work on a Saturday afternoon, mentioned by around one in four. There was also a feeling that, on balance, playing standards had declined. The player football fans would most make a point of going to see was Stanley Matthews.

Further afield, on 3 February, in Cape Town, Mr Macmillan made his famous 'wind of change' speech to the South African Parliament. The following month nearly 70 black Africans were shot during the so-called Sharpeville Massacre. Only three in five of the British public were aware of the Cape Town speech but two in three of these agreed with what had been said. In contrast, almost everyone had heard of the Sharpeville incident and four in five thought that the South African Government's apartheid policy was wrong. At the end of 1959, to measure the impact of the South African boycott campaign, people were asked which of 27 countries they would rather not buy goods from. Then, South Africa was mentioned by 2 per cent and came 19th in the list of the ostracised imports. In March, even before the shooting incidents occurred, South Africa had jumped to 27 per cent and were in second place behind Japan as the unfavoured countries.

March also saw much activity over defence and disarmament matters: first a comprehensive Western disarmament plan was published; Crossman resigned from Labour's Front Bench over the party's defence policy; and Macmillan visited the United States for H-test ban talks. Naturally, defence topped the list in March of important problems thought to be facing the country. Three in four of the public felt that Britain wanted the Summit Meeting to succeed, three in five felt that America did, and two in five thought that Russia did. Only one in three, however, felt that the summit talks would succeed in reducing world tension. On the question of what Britain itself should do about nuclear weapons, 31 per cent wanted us to continue to make our own nuclear weapons, 26 per cent wanted them to be given up completely, and 19 per cent wanted to pool all nuclear weapons with other NATO countries and rely mainly on American production. By the end of May, satisfaction with Macmillan had risen to 79 per cent, the highest for any prime minister since the war - and 27 years later still not surpassed - though support for the Conservative party remained unchanged. This was after Khrushchev announced a US spy plane had been shot down over Russia and after the collapse of the Summit Conference. Nine in ten put at least some of the blame on the Russians for the collapse but only one in five put all of the blame on them. Very few regarded the Americans as solely to blame but three in four held them to be partially responsible. The events had also seriously weakened the British peoples' trust in both the Russians and the Americans: 47 per cent were less inclined than before to trust the Russians and 44 per cent were less inclined to trust the Americans.

The Bank Rate had been increased from 4 per cent to 5 per cent in January and then raised another point in June. In between, HP restrictions were reintroduced. Despite these economic measures, the balance of opinion was that peoples' standard of living was going up, though their savings were less than six months before. One in two also expected prices to go up in the next six months, the highest figure since 1957. External affairs, however, still dominated domestic affairs in the list of important problems facing the country.

After 22 years' association, the final Gallup Poll commissioned by The *News Chronicle*, soon to disappear from the newsstands, took place in mid-October 1960 and was in fact published in The *Daily Mail* on 20 October. The survey was confined to England and Wales and was a wide ranging survey of attitudes towards the three major parties and the political situation generally. One of the questions which retains its interest for readers in the 1980s dealt with the concept of voters having two votes and asked people who would be their second choice (where the leading party failed to achieve a majority of the votes). The Liberals would have been the party to reap the advantages of such a system had it been in operation: three in five Conservatives and two in five Labour supporters chose the Liberals as their second choice. At the same time, a little over one in three felt that a Lib-Lab coalition would be a good thing, though slightly more thought otherwise.

At the end of October the Conservatives went into a 13 per cent lead over Labour, the latter down to 37 per cent, their lowest level of support since the spring of 1950. In the by-elections in mid-November the Liberals pushed Labour into third place in Carshalton, Ludlow, Petersfield and

Tiverton. Later that month, as more and more short-time working was announced, the economy, particularly unemployment, moved into second place in the list of the important problems facing the country. At the same time, the proportion expecting unemployment to go up over the next six months rose to an all-time high, while perceived business activity declined.

Who or what were the best of 1970? Don Thompson was voted the outstanding sports personality because of his Olympic gold medal, followed by other Olympic athletes: diver Brian Phelps, runner Herb Elliot, and swimmers Anita Lonsborough and Ian Black. For the second year running 'South Pacific' was voted best film of the year, with 'Ben Hur' in second place and 'The Ten Commandments' third. 'Emergency Ward 10' emerged as the best television programme, with two topical magazine programmes - 'Tonight' and 'Panorama' - in second and third positions. 'The Archers', the number one radio programme in 1957 and 1958, repeated its triumph in 1960, followed by 'Family Favourites' and 'Housewives' Choice'.

1961

Voting patterns at the beginning of the year were remarkably static: the levels of support being within a range of 2.5 points range for the first four months, with the Conservatives marginally in the lead. Around two in three were satisfied with Mr Macmillan as Prime Minister, while a little over two in five thought that Mr Gaitskell was doing a good job as Labour leader. Selwyn Lloyd's Budget in April was poorly received by the public, with one in three (33 per cent) thinking it was fair and slightly more (36 per cent) thinking he was doing a good job as Chancellor. Both were the lowest figures then for a post-war Budget. Particularly unpopular was the freedom to raise taxes by up to 10 per cent, the increase in the licence duty on private cars and the power to impose an employee surcharge on employers.

Continuing hostility to South Africa made her decide to leave the Commonwealth in March, following the Commonwealth Prime Ministers' conference. The public were fairly evenly divided on the effect of South Africa leaving the Commonwealth, with around one in four each thinking that it would strengthen the Commonwealth, weaken it, make no difference or were undecided. But it was clear from the survey that as far as the general public were concerned, the opposition was to South Africa's policies and not to the country itself or her people. Three in four wanted to be friendly with South Africa, and one in two felt that South Africans in this country should continue to enjoy the advantages that they had had as members of the Commonwealth. When it came to votes in the United

Nations about apartheid, a little over two in five felt that Britain should oppose apartheid, one in four thought we should be neutral and around one in ten wanted to support South Africa. The Common Market was another foreign policy issue which bubbled along throughout the year. In June, prior to the debate in the House of Commons, a little under one in two said they would approve if the government decided that Britain's interest would best be served by joining, with one in five disapproving. These were almost the same proportions found a year earlier. At the personal level, a little over one in four thought Britain's membership would be a good thing for them, one in five saw it as a bad thing and the remainder either felt it would make no difference or were undecided. Economic considerations, particularly prices and employment, were thought to call for most attention in the discussions. A majority (55 per cent), however, felt that if Britain had to join with other powers, it would be better to join with America, than with Europe (22 per cent).

This latter finding could be due possibly to the reported opposition from the Commonwealth about Britain's membership and to the worsening situation over Berlin. In early June two in three of the British public were aware of the disagreement between the West and Russia, and one half of these thought that it was a very serious problem. Almost one in two thought that the West should keep British forces in Berlin even at the risk of war, though one in four felt that the West should withdraw. A fortnight later one in three wanted to negotiate with the Russians, but almost as many thought Britain should maintain her position. In late July, whereas one in three thought that Russia was winning the cold war, only one in ten thought the West was.

Selwyn Lloyd's Budget in late July, where the Bank Rate was raised to 7 per cent, where a 10 per cent surcharge was put on indirect taxation, and where he urged a wages pause, put Labour into the lead for the first time since the 1959 election. Mr Gaitskell's personal popularity, too, went above Mr Macmillan's. As far as Mr Lloyd was concerned, his July rating was even lower than it had been in April, with one in two thinking that he was doing a bad job. One in three of the public also saw the economic situation as very serious and another one in two as serious. A little over one in two disapproved of the government trying to restrict wage claims as much as possible, for people like teachers and local government employees. Perhaps of greater political importance was the feeling, held by one in two of the public, that the government's policies were mainly concerned with the interests of the Conservative party rather than the country as a whole. The ratings of the government's policies as measured by the Gallup Political Index declined all round - particularly in terms of the economy, education, housing and international affairs. By the end of the year, with the Liberals doing well in by-elections, national support for them went up to 20 per cent, then their best figure since the war.

Racing driver Stirling Moss was voted the outstanding sports personality of the year, with footballer Jimmy Greaves in second place, followed by tennis star Angela Mortimer, and the 1953 sports personality, Stanley Matthews. For the fifth year in succession, 'The Archers' was voted as the best radio programme of the year, with comedy series 'Beyond our Ken' in second place, and two record request programmes - 'Housewives' Choice' and 'Family Favourites' - were third and fourth respectively. The number two film of 1960, 'Ben Hur', moved to the top of the list of favourite films of 1961, followed by 'The Guns of Navarone', 'Saturday Night and Sunday Morning' and 'South Pacific'. On the smaller screen, 'Coronation Street' was voted the best TV programme, with 'Maigret' and 'Sunday Night at the London Palladium' in second and third places respectively.

1962

The Conservatives started the year back on level terms with Labour as support for the Liberals declined, and although Mr Macmillan's popularity was well below his best, he moved ahead of Mr Gaitskell. The public's fear of world war in the summer of 1961 - peaking at 40 per cent - subsided to one in four thinking there was much danger in January. By February Labour had regained the lead over the Conservatives and Mr Gaitskell had closed the gap between himself and Mr Macmillan on personal ratings. Then five by-elections took place in March. In the second of these, at Blackpool North, the Liberals got within 3 per cent of the winning Conservative share of the vote, and on the following day swept to victory in Orpington, with an absolute majority of the votes. A Conservative majority of 14,760 had been turned into a Liberal majority of 7855. On the heels of this triumph the Liberal share of the national voting support rose 10 points to 26 per cent, while support for the Conservatives fell to 33 per cent, leaving Labour with a relatively comfortable lead over the two. Approval of the government's record fell to its lowest level since the 1959 election and Tory support at 33 per cent was the party's lowest since January 1946. The April Budget, though better received than its recent predecessors, did nothing to arrest the decline. The government was thought to be doing too much for the well-to-do, too little for the working class and for people living on small pensions or on small incomes, and on balance doing too little to level up the classes. When asked to name the best thing the government had done over the previous ten years, only one in three could mention anything, compared with twice as many who were able to mention something bad. The best things they had done were thought to be their policies on housing and employment, while the most unpopular policy by far was how they had dealt with the economy.

The pay pause, which initially had been thought to be a good thing by the public, became increasingly unpopular. By June the balance of opinion was that it was a bad thing, two in three felt that it was not fair and a little over one in two thought that it had broken down. In mid-July Mr Macmillan announced a number of changes in his Cabinet and his personal rating dropped to equal his lowest figure. On balance the public felt that he had been right to replace Selwyn Lloyd and Mr Watkinson, and slightly over one in two favoured Mr Butler's appointment as deputy prime minister. When asked to choose a possible successor to Mr Macmillan, Mr Butler topped the poll, mentioned by one in four, twice as many as his nearest rival, the deposed Selwyn Lloyd. A little over one in two of the general public agreed with Messrs. Gaitskell and Grimond that the government should resign and call a general election. Although support for the Liberals at this time had fallen somewhat since the months following Orpington, around two in five said they were likely to vote for the Liberals if they thought the party would get a majority or hold the balance, showing a substantial pool of support for the party.

After Berlin came the Cuban crisis, when America discovered that the Russians were installing nuclear missiles in Cuba. One in ten of the British public felt that America should take military action against Cuba, though more than five times as many thought otherwise. In October one in two rejected America's request to join in a shipping boycott of Cuba, with only one in seven favouring the idea. Three in four, after the crisis passed, thought that President Kennedy had behaved wisely and two in three felt that Mr Khrushchev had done so. At around the same time as the problems in Cuba, other international problems erupted on the other side of the world as border clashes took place between India and China. Naturally, three in four of the British public sympathised with India, while only one in fifty sympathised with China, and more than four in five said that the dispute should be submitted to arbitration. Despite this latter finding, three in five approved of Britain selling arms to India on a 'strictly commercial basis' - ever the shopkeeper!

With hindsight, one should note the sentencing of a Mr Vassall to 18 years' imprisonment on 22 October for spying. Three in five then felt that spies in the Services were a serious menace and could cause much damage. An interim report on Vassal was published on 7 November. The year ended with Labour 9 points ahead of the Conservatives and with Mr Gaitskell 11 points ahead of Mr Macmillan in personal popularity.

Two swimmers, Linda Ludgrove and Anita Lonsborough, topped the list of sports personalities of the year, with cricketer Ted Dexter in third place. For the second year running 'Coronation Street' took the award as best television programme, followed by 'Z Cars', 'The Black and White Minstrel Show' and 'Panorama'. On the radio, the list was still dominated for the sixth year in succession by 'The Archers', again with 'Family Favourites' and 'Housewives' Choice' as runners-up. 'Ben Hur' repeated its triumph of 1961 and was chosen best film of the year, with 'Dr No' and 'The Guns of Navarone' in second and third places respectively.

1963

As the year began, the gap between the two main parties widened: a 9 points lead for Labour in December rose to 13 points in January, and to 15.5 in early February. Almost two in three of the public felt that there should be a general election in the near future. Not since 1951 had so many been in favour of a government going to the country. In January people had been asked whether they approved or disapproved of having a member of the House of Lords as prime minister and by a margin of two to one they disapproved of the idea. On 18 January Hugh Gaitskell died and he was succeeded by Harold Wilson as Labour leader. Three in four of the public thought that he would prove a good leader. At the same time, three out of every five voters felt that the time had come for Mr Macmillan to retire. The choice as to his successor was between Mr Heath and Mr Butler, as far as the public was concerned, with Lord Home in sixth place.

On 21 December 1962 the Skybolt missile from America was cancelled - the Americans were scrapping it - and the fait accompli was for Britain to take America's Polaris missile in its place. Three in four of the public had heard of the Skybolt discussions and over one in three of these blamed the government for not foreseeing the circumstances. One in three of the public - almost one in two of those aware of the events - felt that America had behaved badly. Naturally, seven in ten disapproved of the idea of paying more in taxes to buy American missiles and seven in ten felt that Britain was not treated as an equal partner by the United States in affairs that concerned them both.

January also saw unemployment reaching its highest point since 1947, and more than one in two named economic affairs - presumably employment - as the most important problem facing the country. A little over one in four said that they or a member of their family would be affected by rising unemployment and one in five said that they or their family were already being affected. Only one in three felt that the Government would succeed in curing unemployment. In April, when asked what would be the best arguments that either of the two major parties could use to win more votes, keeping down unemployment topped the list of policies given for both parties.

In May Gallup asked a number of questions about the idea of a wealth tax. Two in five approved of a special tax on anyone owning £20,000 in the way of home, furniture, car, income, etc. and 1.5 per cent thought that they would be personally affected. When the amount of wealth was lowered in the questions to £10,000, approval of a wealth tax fell to 32 per cent, with 4 per cent being affected. A further drop in the amount of wealth to £5000 led to only 20 per cent approving of the tax, with almost as many reckoning that they would be affected.

Back on 22 March, in reply to a question in the House of Commons, John Profumo, the Secretary of State for War, denied that any improper relationship existed with Christine Keeler, who had been sexually involved with a Russian diplomat. On 5 June, Profumo admitted in a letter to misleading colleagues in the House of Commons. Support for the Conservative party fell 7 points in a month and Labour went into a 20.5 points lead. Macmillan's personal popularity fell 6 points at the same time, putting him 19 points behind Wilson. Two in five felt that Mr Macmillan should retire and seven in ten thought that an election should be called. While one in two felt that Mr Macmillan had not succeeded in defending his handling of the Profumo case, a little over one in two approved of the way Labour had handled it. Two in three thought that the steps being taken over the security aspects of the case were not sufficient and three in five saw the security aspects as the angle Labour should concentrate on in the House of Commons debate, though one in four thought they should also bring in the moral aspects. A little over one in two felt that cabinet ministers should lead private lives above reproach, but one in three thought that they could lead private lives as they wished. In mid-July almost one in two thought that it would be a good thing for the country if Mr Macmillan resigned. Another month later, the vast majority of people disapproved of newspapers paying large sums to people like Christine Keeler to publish their stories.

On 26 September the Denning Report on the Profumo affair was published. The public was almost evenly divided on whether or not it had cleared members of the government of serious misdemeanors, though one in two took a charitable view of Mr Macmillan and other members of the government, feeling that they were justified in accepting Mr Profumo's denial of an association with Miss Keeler. Almost two in three thought that Mr Macmillan should retire and the top three choices as his successor were Mr Butler, Lord Hailsham and Mr Maudling. Lord Home was in seventh place. On 8 October Mr Macmillan entered hospital for an operation, and he resigned two days later. On the same day, Lord Hailsham renounced his peerage. There can be little doubt that Butler was the politician the public most wanted to see succeed Mr Macmillan - he obtained almost double the support of any other Conservative personality. The public's reaction to Sir Alec Douglas-Home, therefore, was relatively poor: only slightly more being satisfied with him as were dissatisfied. On the other hand, Mr Wilson's personal popularity as Labour leader reached 67 per cent, the highest post-war level (as at 1987) for the main opposition leader. In spite of this disparity in the ratings of the respective leaders, however, the gap between the parties narrowed and the Conservatives ended the year 8 points behind Labour.

Athlete Dorothy Hyman was named sports personality of the year, with racing driver Jim Clark in second place and two footballers - Jimmy Greaves and Dennis Law - third and fourth respectively. For the third year running, 'Coronation Street' took the award as the best television programme, followed by other old faithfuls, 'The Black and White Minstrel Show', 'Panorama' and 'Tonight'. After six years as the public's favourite radio programme, 'The Archers' dropped to second place, ousted by a long-term competitor 'Housewives' Choice'. In third place was 'Beyond our Ken', with 'Family Favourites' in fourth place. On the silver screen, film of the year was 'The Longest Day', followed by the Bond movie 'From Russia with Love', 'Tom Jones' and 'The Great Escape'.

Between the middle of December 1963 and late January 1964, Gallup conducted a major study for ABC Television in three of the main ITV regions: London, the Midlands and the North. The survey, later published as 'Television and Religion' by the University of London Press, was particularly concerned with aspects of audience research in religious television, but also touched upon morality, birth control, racialism and sexual matters. Around three in four, for example, said that on the previous Sunday they had watched television or read a Sunday newspaper. Only one in ten claimed to have gone to church on that Sunday. One in three, however, when shown a list of five occupations, said that the vicar (34 per cent) had the most influence for good in a community, closely followed by a doctor (32 per cent). Bottom of the five was a Member of Parliament, with just 11 per cent thinking they had such influence. A little under one in two said that they watched religious services on television and two in five said that they did not watch them but felt that they were useful for some people. A little under two in five thought that watching religious services on television was a substitute for going to church for people who could not go, and one in four felt that both the BBC and ITV put on such programmes because they had to.

In terms of morality, one third thought that in today's world a person could succeed and always be honest, but three in five thought that it was sometimes necessary to be a bit dishonest on some occasions in order to succeed. Two in three also approved of, or were not worried about, people who had a small job on the side and did not declare it for income tax purposes, and 39 per cent similarly approved or were unconcerned of somebody taking things, such as stationery from the office or small quantities of material from a factory, for personal use. On the other hand, nine in ten disapproved of drink and driving, and disapproved of 'litter bugs'. On homosexuals and prostitutes, 26 per cent and 39 per cent respecively said that they should be punished by law, while around one in four thought that they should be condemned but not punished, and one in three felt that they should be tolerated. Eighty-five per cent said that if they were in the United States they would support the campaign for equal rights for negroes.

When it came to religion as an 'institution', two in five thought that it could answer all or most of today's problems, but slightly more saw it as being largely old-fashioned and out of date. People were more one-sided on the influence of religion on British life: 23 per cent thought it was increasing, while almost three times as many (64 per cent) thought its influence was decreasing. What did people think of regular churchgoers? One in two thought that most people who went to church or chapel regularly were slow to accept new ideas but around three in four accepted that they were sincere in their beliefs. Three in four also thought that the lives of churchgoers were no better than the lives of people who did not go to church, and a little over one in two felt that their lives were no happier, but one in three thought that regular churchgoers did lead happier lives. Around two in five said that they believed in God and the same proportion believed in some sort of spirit or vital force which controlled life. Far fewer, only 28 per cent, believed that there was a devil. While two in three believed that Jesus Christ was the son of God, 16 per cent felt that he was just a man and 5 per cent said they he was just a story. One in two believed that there was life after death, though one in five thought otherwise.

1964

The election year unfolded with Labour 11 points ahead of the Conservatives and Sir Alec 16 points behind Mr Wilson in personal popularity. Almost one in two felt that Labour would win the next election, while a little over one in four gave the Conservatives a chance. Despite these distinct advantages for Labour, the Conservatives were thought best able to handle the problem of Britain running into economic difficulties (a 12 points lead) and to best handle foreign affairs (a 20 points lead). The latter was no doubt a reflection of Sir Alec's background, but in the event of a straightforward television meeting between the two party leaders, Wilson was thought to be the one who would come out best from such a programme.

Rather prematurely, on 6 February, it was announced that a railway tunnel under the Channel was to be built: a decision three in five of the public approved of. Three weeks later the Bank Rate was raised from 4 per cent to 5 per cent, nine days after the biggest trade gap for more than a century. A modest recovery for the Conservatives was thus reversed, while Sir Alec's personal rating continued to decline.

Back in late December, violence broke out in Nicosia, Cyprus. After a temporary calm, the fighting intensified and more British troops were sent to the island. The public were ill-informed as to what was to happen about Cyprus: fewer than one in three said that they were aware of new plans for its future. One in two also felt that if Cyrpus had to be policed by troops, the United Nations should be given the problem - a recurring British response. When asked in late February what should be done if the UN was unable to solve the problem, one in three thought that Britain should stay on the island and use as many troops as necessary, but almost one in two felt that we should pull out and let the Greeks and Turks fight it out between themselves. By the end of March around one in two approved of the government's handling of the situation, but one in four disapproved. In May around three in four felt that Britain was carrying too much of the burden in Cyprus.

The April Budget was poorly received by the public with more seeing it as not being fair as thought that it was fair. Around one in two felt that Mr Maudling was doing a good job as Chancellor, but the problem was, however, that substantial majorities felt that the Budget would not bring prices down in the shops, would not encourage people to go out and spend money in the shops, would not make it easier for people to manage, would not encourage people to work harder and would not help the Conservatives to regain lost votes. The gap between the two major parties widened and support for Labour rose to 55 per cent, their highest level since the war.

The year witnessed a number of disturbingly violent incidents at seaside resorts during the summer, starting in Clacton over the Easter holiday, involving bands of teenagers. More than nine in ten of the public became aware of the Clacton incidents and one in two of these felt that the incidents were serious, though one in three thought that they had been exaggerated by the newspapers. Heavier penalties, mentioned by one in two of the public, was their main answer to the problem, though one in five thought that parents should be made more responsible for their children. Further such incidents occurred over the Whitsun weekend in Margate and Brighton, and the public reacted in a similar way to Clacton; Hastings and Great Yarmouth suffered over the August bank holiday weekend. By then, two in three of the public saw such incidents as serious and two in three wanted heavier penalties for the unruly teenagers. Naturally, although one in five said that they felt sorry for the teenagers, three times as many were cross with them. On a less violent, though related, topic, three in four of the public disapproved of women wearing topless bathing suits.

As the summer passed and the October election came closer, Labour's massive leads melted, so that single figure differences became more the pattern. The final Gallup Poll had the margin down to just 3.5 per cent - Labour won the election by 1.8 per cent.

5 1964 - 1970: The Wilson Era

The public reacted positively to Labour's victory in the election - it had after all been due to their voting preferences - with four in ten saying that the result would affect them favourably and two in ten unfavourably. In the week leading up to polling day people had been asked which of a number of policies Labour would have been elected to implement, if they won. Top of the 13 items was raising old age pensions (63 per cent), followed by control the price of building land (46 per cent), nationalise steel and water supplies (43 per cent) and to repeal the Rent Act (40 per cent). Three in four of the public thought that Harold Wilson would be a good prime minister, while they were, on the other hand, evenly divided on whether or not Sir Alec Douglas-Home should carry on as leader of the Conservative party. If he had retired, Mr Butler and Mr Maudling were the public's choice as his successors.

Why had people voted the way they did? Asked to rate the importance of nine reasons, Britain's position in the world came top with 46 per cent saying that it was 'very important', followed by their income (39 per cent), Britain's military strength (38 per cent) and their children's future (33 per cent). None of which one would normally link with Labour's strengths. Labour in the closing months of 1964 went from a slim 1.8 per cent lead in the election to leads in excess of 10 points. Around six in ten were satisfied with Mr Wilson as prime minister, while more people thought Sir Alec was not proving a good leader of the Conservative party than thought he was. Mr Grimond was doing even better, with two in three thinking he was doing a good job as Liberal leader. With Labour's narrow majority in mind, people were asked in late October which of Labour's plans they were entitled to go ahead with. Nine in ten said they should increase old age pensions, 81 per cent were in favour of them stepping up school building and 71 per cent of giving incentives to businessmen to encourage exports. Two in three also thought that Labour should set up planning boards to increase production and to take the initiative to try for an international agreement to prevent the further spread of nuclear weapons. On the other hand, a majority (56 per cent) felt that Labour should not go ahead with nationalising steel; slightly fewer (47 per cent) thought Labour should not change Britain's nuclear defence policies; and 39 per cent were against giving back to trade unions the right to threaten a strike without fear of legal action. Only one in four wanted another election in the near future, while six in ten thought that the government should carry on.

MPs' salaries were raised to £3250 a year in mid-November. A majority (56 per cent) thought that they should get an increase but as many (55 per cent) felt that the new salary was too high, and even more (62 per cent) thought that the increase should be postponed rather than be implemented immediately. This was at a time when the Bank Rate was raised from 5 per cent to 7 per cent, income tax was raised in an autumn Budget, as well as petrol being increased by 6d (2.5p) a gallon. A majority (55 per cent) thought that the country had a serious economic situation but 63 per cent felt that the government was handling the situation properly.

At the same time a number of social questions were asked, the first dealing with race relations. People were asked how they would react to both coloured people and Jewish people in a number of social situations. On average, less than 5 per cent said that they 'would be pleased' to have either as a neighbour, friend, friend to their children, workmate, employer or in-law, with Jews being slightly more acceptable than coloured people. This latter phenomenon was also true about the proportions saying they 'would not mind'. As a neighbour, for example, 71 per cent said they would not mind a Jew, compared with 44 per cent for a coloured person, and as a friend the replies were 50 per cent and 40 per cent respectively. Antipathy to both groups was highest on the question of having one as a son-in-law or daughter-in-law, though again there were significant differences. Whereas 9 per cent said they 'would strongly dislike' a Jew as an in-law, the proportion rose to 44 per cent for a coloured person. On another topic, at the time of writing this section, English football clubs were still waiting to be allowed to play in European fixtures. Two figures from November 1964 will show that little changes. Then only 17 per cent of the public felt that the Football Association was being firm enough in its handling of players who played rough and even fewer (10 per cent) said they were being firm enough with clubs who did not keep their spectators under control.

In the wider sphere, more people (44 per cent) wanted Britain to try to join the Common Market than wanted the idea dropped altogether (28 per cent), but the public were almost evenly divided on whether we should continue with the Anglo-French Concorde project or abandon it. The public were also evenly divided on the idea of a NATO navy if it meant giving Germany a share in the handling of nuclear weapons.

At a down-to-earth level, athletes in an Olympic year - Mary Rand, Ann Packer, Robbie Brightwell and Lyn Davies - dominated the list of sports personalities of the year, with a woman heading the list for the third year in succession. For the fourth year running 'Coronation Street' was the public's favourite TV programme, followed by 'The Plane Makers', another ITV programme. The most popular film of 1964 was 'Goldfinger', followed by 'Tom Jones' and another Bond movie, 'From Russia with Love'.

1965

The year began badly for the Labour government, an 8 per cent lead being cut to zero in a week, though Mr Wilson's personal popularity was around 20 points above that of Sir Alec Douglas-Home's. By the end of the month, in contrast to early January, one in two of the public felt that the Conservatives would win the next election. At the beginning almost one in two thought that Labour would emerge victorious again. On 14 January a mass rally took place in London by aircraft workers. Three in five of the public at the time felt that the aircraft industry was very important for Britain, though they were less positive about the industry's efficiency. While 43 per cent thought that it was efficient, 30 per cent thought otherwise. In 1958 the figures had been 52 per cent and 16 per cent respectively. Naturally, three in four of the British public, given the choice between buying cheaper American aircraft or buying British, chose the patriotic option, particularly if the American alternative might damage the British aircraft industry. One in two of the public were also hostile to the idea of an amalgamation of the British and French aircraft industries. Despite increases in confectionery prices, increased postal charges and a rise in mortgage rates, one in two (48 per cent) felt that Britain was moving towards prosperity. This was in contrast to just two years before when only 26 per cent had done so. A little over one in two (55 per cent) also felt that Britain's prospects in the future were better than most other countries.

As a precursor to the now fashionable idea of tactical voting, people were asked a month before the by-election in Roxburgh whether they would approve or disapprove if Labour did not put up a candidate in an attempt to give the Liberals a better chance of winning. While one in three approved of such a policy, slightly more (40 per cent) disapproved. In the event, Labour's share of the votes dropped 4.5 per cent to 11.3 per cent and the Liberals took the seat from the Conservatives with an increase in their share of the votes of over 10 points.

On 11 February the General Services Committee of the BMA recommended the Council to advise all GPs to give three months notice to leave the National Health Service. Immediately following this Gallup asked a number of questions of both the general public and of GPs themselves. As far as the public were concerned, their sympathies lay solidly with the doctors: four in five were satisfied with the treatment they got under the NHS and thought that their NHS doctor did everything they could to give an efficient service. A little over one in two also felt that the family doctors were justified in their claim, sympathised with them rather than with the authorities, but felt that they should not carry out their threat to withdraw from the NHS. On the other hand, almost three in four GPs supported the recommendation of the BMA Committee and said that they were willing to withdraw their services from the NHS. Naturally, nine in ten said that compared with consultants they were not so well treated under the NHS. The overwhelming majority (85 per cent) of GPs felt that the number of doctors in training should be increased and, perhaps alarmingly, more than one in five of them had serious thoughts about emigrating. The public's sympathies were still with the doctors a month later and they suggested that an NHS doctor should be paid around £2900 per annum.

In April White Papers on a prices and incomes policy and on steel nationalisation were published. The former came at a time when one in four of the public thought the economic situation was very serious and another one in two saw it as serious. The balance of opinion, however, was that the government would succeed in dealing with the situation and the previous Conservative administration was thought to be mainly responsible for the state of the economy. By May, though, more people thought that George Brown was doing a bad job (41 per cent) than thought that he was doing a good job (35 per cent). Furthermore, by a margin of two to one, they felt that the wages and prices policy would not be a success. Neither was the government having an easy time on the issue of the nationalisation of steel: a little over one in two of the public in early May thought that the best thing for the future of the steel industry was that it should be put into private hands, with one in three opting for at least partial nationalisation. Almost one in two felt that the Steel Bill should be dropped altogether and another one in five wanted it dropped temporarily. As a consequence, public satisfaction with Mr Wilson as Prime Minister dropped from around the 60 per cent mark in the first four months of 1965 to 48 per cent in May and in June, with a concomitant swing in party support to the Conservatives.

In June, as the war in Vietnam dragged on and escalated, it was announced that Mr Wilson was to lead a Commonwealth peace mission on the Vietnam problem, an initiative which was predicted to end in failure by Chou En Lai, and which was rejected by both Russia and North Vietnam. Two in three of the public approved of the proposal but only one in five felt that the peace mission would succeed. One in two also thought that Mr Wilson was right to send Mr Davies as his personal envoy for talks in North Vietnam but one in five thought that he was wrong. By this time, the British public were evenly divided on what America should do: one in three each felt that they should continue their present efforts in South Vietnam, or pull out, or were undecided.

On 22 July Sir Alec Douglas-Home resigned as leader of the Conservative party and Edward Heath narrowly defeated Reginald Maudling in the first ballot for the leadership, and was the only candidate in the second. The public's initial reaction to the new leader was good: 64 per cent in early August thinking he would prove a good leader and 51 per cent ten days later saying he was. Support for the Conservatives went up to 49 per cent, their highest since the 1964 election, putting them 7.5 per cent ahead of Labour. At around the same time, Mr Callaghan announced new economic measures, which received a mixed reception. The most popular was the proposed cut in defence spending, while the decision not to increase other public spending was the least popular. Of greater popularity was the announcement on 1 August that the number of Commonwealth immigrants was to be limited - almost nine in ten approved of this and one in two felt that Britain had been harmed by Commonwealth immigrants. By September Labour had regained a comfortable lead over the Conservatives, which they held onto through the rest of the year, and while Mr Wilson's personal popularity was on the increase, Mr Heath's remained fairly static.

The public greeted the idea to shift the August bank holiday to the end of August rather than have it at the beginning with typical British reserve: two in five were undecided whether they approved or disapproved, and the remainder were almost evenly divided in their views. They were equally unconcerned about the shift affecting their holidays. Two per cent said they had moved their holidays to the end of August or beginning of September, 3 per cent had moved in the opposite direction, while the overwhelming majority (95 per cent) were unchanged. On 16 September the National Economic Plan was published and two thirds of the public were aware of it when asked ten days later. A majority (57 per cent) thought that the Plan was a good thing for the country, though they were evenly divided on whether they would personally be affected. Only one in four thought that their industry or trade would be affected and two thirds of these felt that it would have an expansionary effect.

The following month was a hectic time for negotiators as they flew to and fro between London and Rhodesia to discuss independence for that country. On 5 November a state of emergency was declared in Rhodesia and 6 days later Mr Ian Smith signed a unilateral declaration of independence. In 1963 the balance of opinion was that it was wrong to withhold independence from the whites-only Rhodesian government, but by mid-October 1965 the opposite was true and, in fact, 60 per cent thought it was right to withhold independence. In the event of the Rhodesians claiming independence against the wishes of the British government, the public's priorities were to refer the whole matter to the United Nations (42 per cent), accept the situation (26 per cent) or impose boycotts (13 per cent). Although the public felt that Mr Wilson's visit to Rhodesia (24-31 October) had helped the situation, it did not, of course, stop Mr Smith's declaration of independence. The public were also in error on whether or not Mr Smith would succeed in his policy of seizing independence. While 27 per cent thought he would, 42 per cent thought otherwise. Naturally, three in four felt that if the Rhodesians were prepared to give up their stand on independence, Mr Wilson should agree to re-start talks with them and three in four felt that Britain should support the idea of a Commonwealth Conference. Only 43 per cent, however, thought that it would achieve anything.

In the end-of-year 'best of' survey, racing driver Jim Clark emerged as the public's choice of sports personality of the year, followed by boxer Cassius Clay and athlete Mary Rand. 'Coronation Street' still dominated the list of the public's favourite television programmes, with 'Steptoe & Son' in second place and 'The Man from UNCLE' third. The top two films in 1965 were 'The Sound of Music' and 'Mary Poppins', with 'Goldfinger' in third place.

1966

Labour entered 1966 with a 4.5 per cent lead over the Conservatives and with a majority of the public thinking that they would win the next General Election, then just a matter of months away. The public had also become more hawkish on Rhodesia, with 59 per cent thinking that Mr Smith would not succeed. By February Labour's lead had been extended to 9 points and increased further to 11 in March. Harold Wilson was seen as having a strong, forceful personality (54 per cent) and to be both sincere (45 per cent) and experienced (44 per cent). The rating levels he achieved on these three dimensions were all above Mr Heath's best characteristic - sincerity (38 per cent). Another 30 per cent thought him experienced, and 28 per cent thought he had a strong personality. Mr Wilson was also thought to be the person who would come out best from a television debate between himself and Mr Heath. In terms of issues at the election, prices, pensions,

pensions, employment and the National Health Service were rated as the most important in deciding which party people would support. On each of these four issues, among others, Labour was seen as the best party to handle the problem. Two in three of the public thought that Labour would win the election.

That the election was almost a presidential one can be seen in the replies to questions put soon afterwards. When asked why Labour had won and why the Conservatives had lost, 'Mr Wilson' was the main answer given to the former question and 'Mr Heath' the main reason for the latter. Similarly, although around four in five said that they had seen the two leaders on television, 59 per cent felt that Mr Wilson's appearances had helped to increase support for his party, while only 19 per cent felt that Mr Heath had helped his. The growing impact of television on the electorate could also be seen in the post-election surveys. In 1964 71 per cent had watched a party political broadcast for one of the parties and just 18 months later the proportion had risen to 82 per cent.

In late April reactions to the Queen's Speech were measured and majorities of the public approved of seven of the eight main proposals. The eighth proposal, which the public disapproved of by a margin of almost two to one, was to nationalise the steel industry. As it happens, this was the first time that the opening of the new session of Parliament was televised. On 3 May the Budget's main proposal was the Selective Employment Tax (SET), followed on 4 May by substantial pay increases for doctors and dentists and by a seaman's strike on 16 May. From the beginning the public was on the side of the seamen rather than the employers (48 per cent and 14 per cent respectively) and was critical of the government for not doing enough to settle the dispute, though this changed once a court of enquiry was set up. Almost three in four (72 per cent) of the public felt that the seamen should accept the compromise of the Pearson Report and two in three agreed with Mr Wilson that a political group had been responsible for the strike lasting so long. Three in four also felt that there should be a court of enquiry after the strike into the part political groups played in trade union affairs.

Of some current topical interest, and also more than 20 years ago, was the end of the Moors Murder trial on 6 May. A majority (56 per cent) of the public thought that there had been more cases of murder since the death penalty had been abolished - 8 per cent said there had been fewer - and even more, 76 per cent, felt that the death penalty should be re-introduced.

In July the Prices and Incomes Bill, and a bill for the re-nationalisation of steel, was published, the Bank Rate was raised to 7 per cent and further economic measures were introduced. An 18 points lead for Labour in May melted away and by August the Conservatives held a slim half point advantage. At the same time, the personal popularity of Harold Wilson fell by 17 points and Edward Heath's by 12. By then the Labour government topped the list of people who were blamed for the economic situation, though the previous Conservative administration was second. The public also disagreed with Mr Callaghan's claim that the government's measures would restore Britain's balance of payments in 1967 and the Chancellor's personal rating fell from 61 per cent in May to 43 per cent in late July.

How did the British public see themselves in the summer of 1966? Around one in two thought that they were conscientous, cheerful, easy-going, sympathetic, hard-working and kind. Women tended to see themselves as conscientous, kind and sympathetic to a greater degree than men, while men were more likely to say that they were ambitious, active yet relaxed. A majority (59 per cent) of the public in August approved of the French system that gave police the power to take away licences and to confiscate cars on the spot of drivers who had committed serious traffic offences. Even more approved of the reforms in the jury system to allow 10 to 2 majority verdicts in criminal cases (72 per cent) and disqualifying convicted criminals from sitting as jurors (84 per cent).

In late September, when asked how serious was the economic situation, one in two said that it was very serious, double the proportion in April 1965. The government and the trade unions were top of the list of answers to a question on who was mainly responsible for the economic situation. One in two felt that the Steel Bill should be dropped altogether, while a further 22 per cent thought it should be dropped temporarily. After its initial relatively positive response to the prices and incomes policy, the public became less enthusiastic as the summer passed. Whereas in August the policy was thought to be a good thing by a margin of two to one, the ratio had changed to almost an even division of opinion by late September. Over the same period the proportion thinking that the policy was a fair one dropped from 50 per cent to 40 per cent, while the proportion thinking that they would be disadvantaged rose from 31 per cent to 42 per cent.

In the wider field of international relations, Gallup asked a number of questions in the summer of 1966. Closer to home, seven in ten said that they would approve if the government were to decide that Britain's interests would best be served by joining the European Common Market. On the other hand, a majority (55 per cent) felt that Spain, then not a member, did not have a well-based claim to Gibraltar and a little over one in three (37 per cent) thought that we should tell Spain that we could not alter the situation. Slightly more (40 per cent), however, thought that Britain should try to reach a compromise settlement with Spain, though not one suspects where the Spanish would control Gibraltar. Majorities also felt that Britain was in the right over Gibraltar (58 per cent) and that the government was not being tough enough in its negotiations with Spain. Three in five of the public thought that Britain should support NATO, compared with the one in five who favoured the French approach of greater independence. On 7 November the Road Safety Bill was published and, following its publication, people were asked about breath alcohol tests. The vast majority (83 per cent) approved of roadside testing where a motorist had been involved in a serious accident, 59 per cent approved where the motorist had been suspected of a traffic offence, but only 36 per cent approved of a motorist being stopped and tested for some other reason. The same proportion (36 per cent) said they would approve of extending the Bill's proposals to allow police to stop motorists at random to give them breath tests. This is in sharp contrast to the 71 per cent who thought that the government was not being strict enough in dealing with the problem of drink and driving. On a question of changing over to driving on the right, only 29 per cent supported the idea, while more than twice as many (64 per cent) opted for the status quo. A later Law Commission suggestion that it should be made possible to get a divorce by agreement between the two parties was approved of by one in two of the public, with a little over one in three disapproving. The government also decided at that time to make a new approach towards Britain joining the Common Market, though 3 per cent of the public thought that Britain was already a member! In contrast to early 1963, when only slightly more chose the Common Market than chose a closer association with America, a majority (56 per cent) in November 1966 wanted to join Europe. The public were also optimistic about Britain's chances of joining, 58 per cent thinking there was a good chance, but 23 per cent rated our chances as poor. Almost one in three, however, of the public were sceptical of Mr Wilson's motives, thinking it was just a political move on his part, though one in two felt that he really wanted Britain to join.

'The Sound of Music' was voted as Film of the Year for the second year running, followed by 'Dr Zhivago' and 'My Fair Lady' (the fourth most popular film of 1965). After five years as the most popular television programme, 'Coronation Street' dropped a place to number two, the top position being taken by a new series, 'The Power Game'. In third place was 'Peyton Place', followed by 'The Likely Lads' and 'Till Death us do Part'. The list of sports personalities for 1966 was dominated by England's World Cup Football success, with Bobby Moore and Bobby Charlton as the two most popular personalities, with England's team manager, Alf

Ramsey, in fourth place and Nobby Stiles in fifth. The odd one out, in third place, was boxer Cassius Clay.

The year 1966 had ended with a flurry of activity to do with Rhodesia and Gallup asked people whether they approved or disapproved of the decision to refer the problem to the United Nations. On balance the public approved of the decision - by a margin of 45 per cent to 31 per cent - but two in three (69 per cent) said they would disapprove if the United Nations' measures included the use of force. In the event of the Rhodesians being prepared to give up their stand on independence, 40 per cent said Britain should accept Mr Smith and his government as the official government, but almost as many (36 per cent) thought we should not.

1967

January had hardly got underway before train drivers were threatening a work-to-rule but, luckily for commuters, this was called off a week later. On the 17th Mr Grimond resigned as leader of the Liberal party, to be replaced by Jeremy Thorpe. One in two felt that Mr Thorpe was a good choice and one in three (35 per cent) thought that the Liberal vote would go up at the next election rather than go down (11 per cent). The Prime Minister was buzzing across Europe in the first round of the Common Market talks and Labour started the year 3 points ahead of the Conservatives, increasing its lead in February to 11.5 per cent. At the same time Mr Heath's personal popularity fell to his all-time low as leader of the opposition - 24 per cent in February - and lower than any previous leader.

In January the public were asked their attitudes to the Plowden Report on 'Children and their Primary Schools'. On the whole the Report was favourably received, with some of the proposals achieving almost unanimous approval: around nine in ten, for example, approved of the recommendations that school buildings should be improved, the maximum size of primary school classes should be cut to about 30, and that top priority should be given to schools in poor districts. Eight in ten approved of steps to get parents more fully involved in their children's schooling, seven in ten approved of the greater use of 'teachers' aids', and six in ten approved of the expansion of nursery schooling. Around one in two also approved of starting secondary schooling at 12 instead of 11, and that primary schooling should start in the September term following a child's fifth birthday. Two recommendations had as many disapproving as approving: that children should be allowed to attend school for half a day only until the age of 6, and that corporal punishment should be abolished in primary schools.

In early March, for the first time, people were asked about local authorities selling council houses to the tenants and three in four said that they approved of the idea. In answer to a question in February, council housing came second in the list of priorities for the building industry. Top came hospitals (64 per cent), followed by council housing (39 per cent) and schools (26 per cent). At about the same time the government's Decimal Coinage Bill was published, proposing that the £ should be the main unit of currency in the decimal system. Both before and after publication of the Bill, the public's view ran counter to the government's. By margins of around five to three and two to one, the public favoured the 10/- (50p) as the unit, with the advantage of a lower smallest unit.

The Budget of 1967 contained no big changes and was relatively well received, with a little over one in two thinking James Callaghan was doing a good job as Chancellor (51 per cent) and that the Budget was a fair one (56 per cent). There were doubts, however, about what would be achieved by the Budget. Although a majority felt that the government had done all it reasonably could to protect the £ from the threat of devaluation, majorities, on the other hand, thought that it would not encourage people to work harder nor would it help to keep prices down. A Labour lead of 11.5 points in February melted away and by April, after the Budget, the Conservatives took a 4 points lead, which continued to improve.

On 2 May Mr Wilson announced that Britain was to apply to join the Common Market. Six days later there was a debate in the House of Commons on the issue, the government winning with a majority of 426. Thirty-five Labour MPs, however, voted against the government and 7 parliamentary private secretaries were subsequently dismissed for abstaining in the vote. A week later President de Gaulle took a firm line against Britain's membership under the present conditions. Before the President's 'non' the public were in favour of joining, though three in four felt that Britain's membership would lead to an increase in food prices. Two in five also took the view that Britain would take a back seat to one of her European partners, primarily France, though one in two thought all the countries would be equal and one in ten saw Britain as the leader.

On 5 June, after various beligerent acts throughout the Middle East, fighting broke out between Israeli and Arab forces, and the Six-Day War began. The British, by a margin of ten to one, sided with the Israelis and tended to blame the Arabs for actually starting the fighting. Their estimates of how long the conflict would last were woefully at odds with the lightning Israeli offensive: only 7 per cent thought it would last for a few days, 26 per cent thought it would last for a few weeks, and 35 per cent felt it would go on for longer. On balance they felt that the Israelis would come out on top in the fighting. When asked what Britain should do, two in five said we should work with other countries to stop the fighting, while one in three just wanted to sit on the sidelines doing nothing, and one in five opted to support Israel. Only one in a hundred were prepared to join sides with the Arabs. On the domestic front, three in five approved of the way the government had handled the situation and around two in three felt that petrol rationing would not have to be enforced in Britain. By mid-July, however, the proportion thinking that there would be petrol rationing had increased from 14 per cent to 35 per cent.

Also in mid-July, a government report recommended that the legal age of majority should be lowered from 21 to 18. A few weeks later Gallup interviewed a sample of 18-20 year olds on their reaction to the report. Four in five had heard or read about it and three in five of these felt that the Committee had done a good job. On perhaps the main recommendation in the report, a little over one in two (56 per cent) agreed that the voting age should be reduced to 18, though 30 per cent disagreed and only two in three said that they would bother to vote. One in three did not know which party they would support if they voted, but Labour had a 7.5 points advantage among those who did give a preference. Majorities of these young people approved of men and women aged 18 and over being able to inherit property (75 per cent), make a will (69 per cent) and marry without their parents' consent (58 per cent). They were more evenly divided on the question of being able to get a mortgage and on furnishing their home on hire purchase: one in two approved but one in three disapproved. One in two of the young adults said that they would like to emigrate to another country, with Australia, Canada, New Zealand and the USA as their favourite destinations.

In October, for only the second time since the election, Mr Heath's personal rating rose above that of Mr Wilson, and at the same time the Conservatives took an 11 points lead over Labour. One in two thought that the government should go to the country, though one in three felt that they should carry on, and three times as many saw the Conservatives winning such an election as thought Labour would. When asked which of the two party leaders would make the better prime minister the public was evenly divided, whereas in March 1966 Mr Wilson had led Mr Heath by almost two to one. In party terms the Conservatives were seen to be the party to best handle the problems of the economy, full employment, strikes and taxation. They were also thought to have forward-looking plans for improving British standards of living. Furthermore, in the disputes with the railway guards, building workers and dockers, the public sided with the employers in each case. While the government wrestled with the problem of staving off devaluation, though for not very much longer as it happened, the public were optimistic in thinking that devaluing the £ could be avoided. On the other hand, if sterling were to be devalued, two in three of the public felt that they would suffer, only one in five thought that it would help Britain to strengthen her economic position, and two in five thought that the government should resign. The subsequent devaluation in November led no doubt to the breaking of a record in the opinion polls. In The *Daily Telegraph* on 27 November, Gallup gave the Conservatives a 13 per cent lead - one of the biggest found in favour of the party in the previous 30 years - increasing to 17.5 per cent in December, its biggest lead since the war.

At about the same time, in early December, people were asked which of two dozen words they thought best described the French, Chinese, Germans, Japanese, Americans and Russians. Our impressions of the French and Chinese were not particularly strong, as measured by the vocabulary employed: the highest mention for the French, for example, was that they were 'quick-tempered', mentioned by 14 per cent, followed by 'ordinary' (12 per cent), 'artistic', 'conceited' and 'religious' (11 per cent each). The top answers for the Chinese were that they were 'warlike' (18 per cent), 'hard-working' (17 per cent), 'sly' (15 per cent) and 'treacherous' (10 per cent). On the other hand, a little over one in three saw the Germans as being 'hard-working' (35 per cent), 'practical' (15 per cent), 'intelligent' (13 per cent), 'arrogant' but 'progressive' (12 per cent each). The Japanese, too, were thought to be 'hard-working' (30 per cent) and 'progressive' (18 per cent), but like the Chinese, 'cruel' (13 per cent), 'warlike' (11 per cent) and 'treacherous' (10 per cent). A little over one in eight (13 per cent) thought that they were 'intelligent'. The characteristics most often attributed to the Americans were that they were 'progressive' (24 per cent), 'conceited' (16 per cent), 'intelligent', 'generous' (15 per cent each) and 'hard-working' (14 per cent). 'Hard-working' topped the list of Russian stereotypes with 33 per cent, followed by 'progressive' (23 per cent), 'intelligent' (15 per cent) and 'practical' (11 per cent). When asked about countries rather than their people and asked to choose between France and Germany as our chief ally, more than twice as many chose Germany (49 per cent) as chose France (22 per cent).

Britain's rapid decline as a world power could be seen in the replies to other questions at the same time. In January 1965, when asked which country, apart from the three super-powers, had the most influence in world affairs, Britain came top with 39 per cent, with France in second place (17 per cent). By December 1967 the figures were almost reversed, with France leading (37 per cent) and Britain second (24 per cent). America was still regarded as Britain's best friend in the world though she had dropped from 59 per cent in 1965 to 45 per cent. In 1963 Britain's best friends in Europe were thought to be Denmark (12 per cent) and Holland (11 per cent). By 1967 the top three were Germany (18 per cent), Holland (14 per cent) and Denmark (11 per cent). This was, of course, against a background of a negative reaction to de Gaulle on Britain's membership of the Common Market and the inevitable French veto.

In the annual round-up of the best of the year, 'The Sound of Music' was voted as the best film for the third year running, with 'Dr Zhivago' in second place and 'The Dirty Dozen' in third place. 'Coronation Street' returned to its long held place as the most popular TV programme, being top six times in seven years. Second was 'The Frost Programme' and 'Dr Finlay's Casebook' third. For the first time in a decade, a boxer, Henry Cooper was voted Sports Personality of the Year. In second and third places were two Manchester United footballers, Bobby Charlton and George Best. Bobby Charlton was also second in 1966 when England's World Cup team dominated the list.

1968

The year began with a second heart transplant in Cape Town, the first taking place the previous 3 December. There were also new government measures to cut spending on defence and on the social services, and Mr Wilson visited Moscow. It was a boost that he needed for his flagging popularity, down to its lowest since the election at 33 per cent. Only one in four (26 per cent) thought that the government's economic policies would succeed, while almost twice as many (48 per cent) took the opposite view.

On 15 January the Divorce Law Reform Bill was published and Gallup soon after measured the public's initial reaction to the main proposals. On the general question of divorce, the public were fairly evenly divided, with 28 per cent saying leave things as they were, 34 per cent saying that divorce should be made easier, and 27 per cent that it should either be made more difficult or that it should not be allowed at all. Under the Divorce Bill the breakdown of the marriage would be the only grounds for divorce and various facts would have to be proved by the petitioner to establish breakdown of the marriage. Majorities in each case agreed that the following should be included as proof of breakdown:

- that one party has committed adultery and the other finds it intolerable to live with him/her (78 per cent)

- that the partner has behaved in such a way that the one who wants a divorce cannot reasonably be expected to live with him/her (76 per cent)
- that the husband and wife have lived apart for at least 2 years and both agree to a divorce (70 per cent)
- that the husband and wife have lived apart for at least 5 years, even when only one of them wants a divorce (56 per cent)
- that one party has deserted the other without cause for 2 years (56 per cent)

Barely one in two (48 per cent) approved of the central provision in the Bill, that the complete breakdown of the marriage was to be the only grounds for divorce, and 37 per cent disapproved. Naturally, the public felt that if the Bill became law it would lead to more divorces (44 per cent) rather than less (5 per cent). On a question of a couple with a child, eight in ten felt that it was better for the child to live with one divorced parent than to live with unhappily married parents (10 per cent).

Two in three of the public approved of the heart transplant operations taking place in South Africa and in the United States, though 54 per cent felt that there were other needs in British hospitals which should be given priority. A little over one in three (39 per cent) said they would like to see heart transplant operations in Britain and when asked whether they would be prepared to donate their heart or other organs to be used for transplanting after their deaths, 63 per cent said they would. One in four were against the idea and one in ten were undecided. After a temporary decline in January the Conservatives surged to 52.5 per cent in February, putting them 22.5 points ahead of Labour, their best position since the war. Mr Heath's personal rating, however, showed no such improvement and he ran over 20 points behind his party. On the other hand, public pressure was growing for Mr Wilson to retire to make way for another party leader. Whereas 32 per cent in July 1967 thought he should retire, the figure had risen to 45 per cent in late January.

In the international sphere in January US nuclear bombs were lost in Greenland, an American spy ship was seized by the North Koreans and there was a flare-up of Viet Cong activity in Vietnam. Only 19 per cent felt that Britain should send troops to help the Americans if fighting broke out between themselves and the North Koreans, and 69 per cent were opposed to the idea. Even in the event of the United Nations becoming involved, more said that Britain should stay out (49 per cent) than wanted to send troops (39 per cent). Similarly, in the Vietnam situation, almost nine in ten said it was more important for Britain to try to get peace talks going than to support the Americans. Only one in three agreed with Mr Heath's call on the government to back the United States' Vietnam policy. In contrast to the American public one in two (54 per cent) Britons felt that a halt of American bombing in North Vietnam would improve chances for meaningful peace talks. In America the reverse was true, with 70 per cent thinking America's chances were better if the bombing continued.

Mr Jenkins' first Budget on 19 March was not particularly well - received and neither was he personally. The 43 per cent thinking the Budget was a fair one had only been lower under Mr Maudling in 1964, Mr Selwyn Lloyd in 1961, Mr Heathcoat Amory in 1960 and Mr Thorneycroft in 1957. Similarly, the 41 per cent thinking Mr Jenkins was doing a good job as Chancellor was on the low side and was the worst since 1961. More than one in two (57 per cent) said that the Budget had made them less favourably inclined towards the government. Support for the Conservatives rose to 54.5 per cent in April and then peaked at 56 per cent in May - their highest post-war level. Support for Labour at the same time slumped to only 28 per cent, the lowest for either of the major parties, though the Conservatives had been down to 27.5 per cent in February 1945.

On 9 April the Race Relations Bill was published. Beforehand, in mid-March, nine in ten approved of recent restrictions on the number of immigrants, two in three felt that controls on the numbers were not strict enough and one in two thought that the government had handled the issue badly. Studies after the publication of the Bill had bare majorities agreeing that coloured people from the Commonwealth should be allowed to compete for jobs in Britain on equal terms with people born here and vote in British elections, but on balance were against admitting them to council housing lists on the same conditions as British-born. At most, two in five felt that it should be an offence to discriminate against someone on racial grounds in terms of employment, housing and membership of employer or worker organisations. The balance of opinion tended to think that these should not constitute an offence. On 20 April Mr Powell made his 'river of blood' speech in Birmingham, leading to his dismissal from the shadow cabinet, but almost all the public (96 per cent) were aware of the speech, three in four agreed with what Mr Powell had said and two in three felt that Mr Heath was wrong in sacking him. The Race Relations Bill, if anything, worsened race relations in Britain, or at least the public's perception of the situation. Increasing proportions thought that the controls on the number of immigrants were not strict enough and that Britain had been harmed by Commonwealth immigrants. The balance of opinion initially approving of the Bill reversed to one of disapproval and more people thought it would not succeed in protecting the interests of coloured people in Britain than thought it would. More people also said that the race relations in Britain were getting worse and said that their own feelings were becoming less favourable. In May 27 per cent said that immigrants were the most urgent problem facing the country, compared with only 6 per cent in February.

The year 1968 was very much the 'Year of the Students', with student unrest both here and in many other parts of the world. As far as Britain was concerned, only 19 per cent sympathised with the students as to the amount they got in grants and even fewer (15 per cent) on the way the universities were run. Almost two in three (63 per cent) felt that the riots in France could happen in Britain. Naturally, given the choice of spending more educational money on students or on pre-school nurseries, the latter were chosen by a margin of almost three to one over students. A study among students themselves - at Cambridge and Sussex - showed that only a minority of undergraduates had taken part in public demonstrations or protest meetings. In Cambridge it was 21 per cent, rising to 40 per cent of the Sussex undergraduates. The active minority, however, enjoyed the general approval of the majority of their fellow students, and the vast majority felt that there would be more student protests. The part which violence would play in student affairs was also thought to be on the increase in spite of the fact that very few students approved of it. Students at both universities were more concerned about the state of the world at large than they were with events at home or with their own position. Although only a minority of the public sympathised with the students, the public thought they had a lot to complain about. Around two in three of the public also felt that they, the public, did not have enough to say in the way the government ran the country, the way local authorities handled things, the television programmes put out by either the BBC or the ITV, or in the services provided by the nationalised industries. Two in three felt that there should be a referendum system whereby certain issues could be put to the people to decide by popular vote, rather than the government deciding all important issues.

The year 1968 will also be remembered for the Russian invasion of Czechoslovakia. Even before the invasion the public's sympathies were with Czechoslovakia: they thought that Russia had not dealt fairly with her and, on balance, that in the end the Czechs would have to do what Russia wanted. A later study found the balance of opinion thinking that Britain was doing all it could to help Czechoslovakia. It perhaps should also be remembered (or should we say forgotten?) as the year when the Post Office introduced the two-tier letter rate: 5d (about 2p) for first class and 4d (about 1.5p) for second class. Naturally, almost everybody had heard of the new system and four in five disapproved of it. Two in five

(43 per cent) said that they would never use the 5d rate, though they probably do now.

As the summer wore on, Labour recovered some of the ground lost in the spring, cutting back the Conservative advantage to 7.5 per cent in early October but the flow was then reversed with the Conservatives ending the year 25.5 points ahead. Almost certainly this was due to reactions to the imposition of hire purchase restrictions on 1 November and to the mini-Budget on 22 November when the price of petrol, spirits and cigarettes was increased along with purchase tax. Harold Wilson's call for restraint was rejected by the public: while 37 per cent thought restraint was inevitable, more (46 per cent) felt that it could have been avoided if the government had adopted different policies to encourage economic expansion. When asked which party could best handle the problem of maintaining prosperity, the Conservatives had a 15 points advantage over Labour. In answer to another question on what the effect had been of 4 years under Labour, 25 per cent said they were better off but almost twice as many (45 per cent) said they were worse off. A little over one in two (57 per cent) felt that the government's general economic policies would not succeed and 52 per cent took the same pessimistic view of the prices and incomes policy.

One happy note for the end of the year was 'The Sound of Music' being voted Film of the Year yet again, for the fourth year running, with 'Dr Zhivago' in second place, for the third successive year. After 31 years since it first appeared, 'Gone with the Wind' took third place on its re-release. On the smaller screen BBC's 'Forsyte Saga' was the most popular television programme, followed by 'Coronation Street', 'Frost on Sunday' and 'The Dave Allen Show'. As in other Olympic years, the list for Sports Personality of the Year was dominated by Olympic stars. Athletes David Hemmery and Lilian Board came first and third respectively, with show-jumping's Marion Coates in second place.

1969

The year started badly with record absenteeisms in industry, to be followed by a postal strike at the end of the year. In the international sphere Vietnam peace talks re-opened in Paris and, even further afield, the Russians linked two craft in outer space and transferred the crew. Back in Britain, trade union legislation was in the offing and Gallup surveyed people's reactions to possible changes in trade union laws. Six of the proposals included in the study received majority approval:

- workers to be able to appeal against unfair dismissal (85 per cent)

- the government could intervene in unofficial strikes which were likely to harm the national interest (74 per cent)
- union members who defied the law and continued to strike may be liable to be fined (69 per cent)
- a special body would inspect agreements on wages and working conditions, settle specified disputes and speed up wage barganing (66 per cent)
- a secret ballot of members to be held before official strikes (63 per cent)
- a 'cooling-off' period while the ballot was taken (61 per cent)

One item, government grants to assist union mergers, was given the thumbs down by the public with the balance of opinion disapproving. A measure of the government's problems with the labour relations' issue was that the Conservatives were seen as the party to best handle strikes, that Labour would be too weak in their actions against strikes, and that they would not succeed in cutting down strikes.

On 28 January the PAYE pension plan was announced and a little over a fortnight later four in five were aware of the proposals. Three in four felt that the current pension scheme needed to be changed and one in four thought that the proposed scheme would not go far enough. The public to some degree clung to the idea of an egalitarian society, 27 per cent thinking everyone should pay the same amount towards their pension, but 62 per cent felt that you should pay more if you earned more. Naturally a similar pattern of replies emerged on the size of the pension: one in four said that everyone should receive the same pension on retirement, while two in three said those who paid larger contributions should receive a larger pension.

Mr Jenkins' second Budget received a significantly better reaction overall from the public than his first had. The proportion thinking that it was a fair one (59 per cent) had only been surpassed on two occasions, in 1966 and in 1958. The public's rating of Mr Jenkins, however, was only a middling one with 49 per cent thinking that he was doing a good job. Majorities of the public approved of the increased tax on sherry and wines, but disapproved of the increases on petrol and of the Selective Employment Tax. One in two also felt that the proposed increases in pensions were too small.

On 17 April in Northern Ireland, the Ulster Unionist candidate was defeated in a by-election by Bernadette Devlin, standing under a Civil Rights banner. Two days later rioting broke out and British troops were sent to the province to guard key installations. The public were evenly divided on this latter action with two in five each approving and disapproving. In the other direction, across the Channel, President de Gaulle resigned after being defeated in a national referendum. The British public's reaction was one of almost overwhelming glee, with majorities thinking that the resignation would be good for France, good for international affairs generally, and good for Britain's economic position. Slightly further afield, Spain stopped Spanish workers crossing the border into Gibraltar. Naturally two in three of the British public thought that Spain did not have a well-based claim to Gibraltar and one in two felt that people should not take their holidays in Spain.

In mid-July Apollo II was launched and landed a man on the Moon on the 20th, while down on earth Senator Edward Kennedy was involved in an accident in which a young woman died. More than nine in ten of the British public were aware of the latter incident and they took a compassionate view of it. While the balance of opinion was that he should not resign as a senator, the balance was also of the opinion that he should not stand as a candidate for the presidency in the next election.

Gallup conducted a special survey in June on the topic of democracy and what it meant to people. Two in three of the public felt that Britain was a democracy, though one in two thought that we were becoming less democratic. When asked what they understood by 'democracy', one in three said freedom of speech and of the press, while another one in three saw it as meaning individual liberty, one in four thought it meant everyone had a vote and one in five said free elections. One in two thought there were countries who were more democratic than Britain, the top three mentioned being the United States, Australia and Sweden. On the other hand, almost nine in ten mentioned a less democratic country, with the Soviet Union, China, Czechoslovakia and East Germany topping the list. Three in four of the public agreed with the view that what counts today is not what you can do or how hard you work, but who you know and how much influence you have. Only one in three, however, subscribed to the conspiracy theory, that our lives were governed by secret plots of politicians. Slightly more, four in ten, felt that British politicians were looking out more for themselves than their party or the country. On questions about the law and justice in Britain, a little over one in two felt that the judicial system was fair to everyone, and also that the courts dispensed justice impartially. Slightly more, two in three, thought that judges were completely independent of the government of the day and were not influenced by them in any way.

On the domestic political front, a substantial 23.5 points lead for the Conservatives in July declined to a mere 2 points by October, though it was pushed back up to 10.5 per cent in December. The summer was dominated by events in Northern Ireland, with serious rioting in Londonderry on 12 August, spreading to Belfast the following day and eventually leading to the death of five people on 14 August. Five days later British troops took over security. The government gained strong backing from the public for their decision to send in the troops - 67 per cent thought it was right - and for their handling of the situation (57 per cent approving). The public were less charitable in their views on the Common Market, well over half (57 per cent) thinking that Britain should drop the idea of trying to join. This was the highest level of opposition for over six years. There was also an increase in the number who thought that Britain would take a back seat to one of the other members if it joined. Whereas in late 1966 the public, by a margin of four to one, thought that Britain's membership would be a good thing, by November 1969 the margin was two to one thinking it would be a bad thing.

In November people in 17 countries around the world, encompassing North America, South America, Europe, Africa and Asia, people were asked to review the Sixties and to look forward to the Seventies. In Britain, and in fact in most other countries, John F. Kennedy was thought to have been the outstanding personality anywhere in the world in the 1960s, and America followed by West Germany, was thought to be the country which could look back with most satisfaction for what it had achieved. Peace was the main wish people wanted fulfilled in the next decade, mentioned by two in five of the British public. They looked towards the 1970s with a slightly pessimistic view: although 38 per cent felt that the world would be a better place to live in and 24 per cent thought there would be little change, 26 per cent thought that the world would not be so good to live in. Looking ahead ten years, the British thought that the USA would have the highest standard of living and would have the leading position in the field of science. When it came to which country would have the strongest military force, the USA was second by a small margin to Russia. The British gave a very patriotic response to a question on which country would have the most to offer ordinary people for their happiness: one in two said Britain. Finally, people were asked to look even further ahead, 20 years, and to say whether a number of possible events would have occurred. Top of the 12 items was 'a cure for cancer will have been found', predicted by 75 per cent of Britons. Next came a cluster of three items: 'our standard of living will have doubled' (48 per cent), 'expectation of life will have risen to 100 years' and 'we will be working a three-day week' (43 per cent each). A number of international items occupied the middle of the table: 'Russia and the West will be living together peacefully' (37 per cent), 'man will be living on the Moon' (29 per cent), 'you will be able to travel anywhere in the world without a passport' (27 per cent) and 'all countries will have ceased to manufacture H-bombs or anything like them' (24 per cent). The most pessimistic predictions took the bottom places: 'civilisation as we know it will be in ruins' (15 per cent), 'capitalism and the western way of life will have collapsed' (13 per cent), 'Russian communism will have vanished' (12 per cent) and 'an atomic war between Russia and America' (10 per cent). With just a few more years to go, at the time of writing, none of these predictions have come to pass, with the possible exception of peaceful coexistence between Russia and the West.

That 'Sound' still echoed in 1969, with 'The Sound of Music' voted yet again as the top film of the year, followed by another musical, 'Oliver' and, for the fourth year in succession, 'Dr Zhivago'. The top television programme of the year was 'Coronation Street', for the sixth time in nine years. The runners-up were 'Please Sir!', 'The Forsyte Saga' and 'Softly, Softly'. George Best, the Ulster and Manchester United footballer emerged as Sports Personality of the Year, with tennis star Anne Jones in second place and golfer Tony Jacklin third.

1970

The year began with the Conservatives still in the lead, by 7.5 per cent, and still the public's favourites to win the next election. The proportion approving of the government applying to join the Common Market had dropped to 22 per cent, compared with 36 per cent just 3 months earlier. On 14 April Roy Jenkins presented his third and most popular Budget. Two in three of the public thought that it was fair and three in five saw Mr Jenkins as a good Chancellor. Only Mr Butler in 1963 scored a higher rating. Most people appeared to agree with the view that Mr Jenkins had not produced an electioneering Budget and felt that it would be little or no help to them personally. By early May Labour had taken a 7.5 per cent lead over the Conservatives and more than one in two felt that Labour would win the election. At the same time Mr Wilson was enjoying a 21-points advantage over Mr Heath in personal popularity.

With hindsight one can see the cost of living topping the public's list of the urgent problems facing the country, and on the question of which party could best handle the urgent problems the Conservatives were running neck and neck with Labour. Furthermore, four in five disapproved of the way the government was handling the cost of living and prices. One

6 1970 - 1974: The Success and Failure of Mr Heath

When asked immediately after the election why the Conservatives had won and why Labour had lost, one answer emerged to both questions, 'the cost of living', mentioned by around one in four electors. No other reason was given by more than one in ten. The public's initial reaction to Mr Heath as Prime Minister was only marginally better than their rating of him as Conservative leader: their final verdict of him before the election gave him a rating of 28 per cent, rising to 35 per cent after the event, though 29 per cent said that it was too early to say. In contrast, around three in five thought that Mr Wilson was proving a good leader of the Labour party and almost two in three wanted him to carry on, despite the lost election. The Conservatives emerged from the election as the party the public felt could best handle the problems of the economy, defence, education, the Common Market, prices and strikes. Out of 7 issues, Labour was thought to be able to do better on only one - the National Health Service.

On 30 June EEC entry negotiations began, though almost three in five of the public disapproved of the government applying for membership. The public were more evenly divided on the effect of membership on Britain's standard of living, with around one in three thinking it would get higher and the same proportion thinking it would get lower. But almost three in four thought that food prices would rise a lot and two in five felt that the price of other goods would rise a lot. When asked in early October what was the most urgent problem facing the Conservatives when they met at their annual conference, fewer than one in ten mentioned the Common Market. Top of the list were prices and strikes, mentioned by around one in three each.

These two issues had also dominated the replies to a similar question in late August in the run-up to the annual meeting of the TUC, and the public felt that, on balance, there would be more strikes under the Conservatives than there had been under Labour. Around one in five thought that the government would succeed in cutting down strikes but one in two thought otherwise. This attitude, however, was amended in the light of the government's proposals for the reform of trade union law, though the public still took a pessimistic view of its efficacy. Overall, the public approved of the government's plans, by a margin of two to one.

The death of President Nasser of Egypt in late September was thought by the British public to be a blow to hopes of peace in the Middle East, with nearly half thinking that his death made chances for peace less likely. On the other hand, in a survey conducted just before his death, three in five of the public had a bad opinion of him. This was in contrast to the one in two who had a good opinion of Mrs Golda Meir of Israel and to the two in five who had a good opinion of King Hussein of Jordan. The British public continued to sympathise with Israel in the Middle East dispute rather than with the Arab countries, though one in five felt that Israel should withdraw to their original frontier (after the Six-Day War of 1967) and the same proportion thought that they should return most of the Arab territory but that it should retain hold of strategic places like Jerusalem and the Gaza Strip.

In February 1971 Britain was to adopt a decimal currency system, and, as with many other things, the public became cool to the idea as it got nearer. In 1966, for example, 56 per cent had approved of the switch-over but 4 years later approval had dropped to 46 per cent, with almost as many disapproving. On the other hand, a majority of the public, possibly resigned to the inevitable, felt that the changeover should take place as planned.

December took place with a work-to-rule by electricians, leading to blackouts, as well as to an unofficial strike against the government's Industrial Relations Act. Against this background, it was not surprising that a half of the public saw strikes and labour relations as the most urgent problem facing the country, followed by prices. A little over one in four felt that the government's economic policies would succeed and almost one in two thought that wage claims had not been handled firmly enough.

On a lighter note, people were asked what was the best film they had seen in 1970, and ironically 'The Battle of Britain' came top, with 'Ann of the Thousand Days' in second place. On the small screen 'Coronation Street' again came top, for the eighth time in ten years, with 'Morecambe and Wise' and 'Family at War' sharing second place. As in 1967, boxer Henry Cooper was the public's favourite sports personality, with golfer Tony Jacklin in second place, footballer George Best third and Lillian Board fourth. Lillian Board, the athlete who had died of cancer, also figured in the list of women most admired by the public. In first place was the Queen, followed by Mrs Barbara Castle and the deceased Lillian Board. The most admired men were Harold Wilson, Enoch Powell, Edward Heath and Prince Philip.

1971

As the then latest attempt to join the Common Market had failed, Britain could not have looked to the Commonwealth alone for a secure economic future. In the previous decade most Commonwealth countries had moved away from economic dependence on, or interdependence with, Britain, and simultaneously there had been a growing reluctance to regard Britain as the undisputed leader in foreign affairs. But the Commonwealth was still regarded as vital to Britain's place in the world, not so much as the remnant of a vanished Empire, but as the free association of independent peoples. The results of a series of questions on the Commonwealth in January showed that its strength lay in its multi-racial character, while identification of the Commonwealth with the former white dominions was less strong. Naturally, only one in three of the British public felt that Britain should supply arms to South Africa and one in two said that we should not. Furthermore, compared with 1963, when one in three were satisfied with Britain's position in the world, by 1971 only one in four were.

Also in January, a number of questions were asked about smoking and health. The first of these had not been asked since 1958 and showed the dramatic change in public attitudes over the intervening years. Whereas in 1958 a little over one in three accepted that smoking was one of the causes of lung cancer, and slightly fewer disagreed, the proportion accepting the link had doubled to seven in ten by 1971. Similarly, going further back, one in four in 1956 knew someone who was either cutting down or had stopped smoking altogether, and by 1971 the proportion had risen to two in three. Given this change in attitudes, it was understandable that around four in five approved of a health warning on all cigarette packets, and majorities of the public approved of a ban on all cigarette advertising and promotions, and the removal of cigarette machines from public places.

By the time Britain changed over to its now familiar decimal currency, a majority of the public gave it their approval, although perhaps only grudgingly. Two in three thought that it might be easy to use. With just a few weeks to go, however, before the changeover, there was a surprisingly poor awareness of the new coins. Only three in four could correctly name any of the three new coins that were being introduced, with six in ten aware of the new 2 pence coin. Awareness of the equivalent value of new coins in terms of the old currency was also low, with around 50-60 per cent correctly identifying each of the three coins. Of perhaps greatest impact was the result of the final question, with one in three expecting prices in the shops to go up 'a lot' as a consequence of the changeover and another one in two expecting them to go up 'a little'.

Mr Barber's first full Budget as Chancellor of the Exchequer was both a notable personal success and also brought some welcome relief to his party in public support. From January, when Labour were ahead by 4.5 points, the Conservatives fell behind by 12 points in mid-March, but had reduced the deficit to only 3.5 points following the Budget. But the public were still not convinced that the government could succeed with their economic policies and the great majority felt that not enough was being done to try to stop the rise in prices. By May Labour had regained a 12-points lead. At the same time, with unemployment running around the 800,000 mark, it was second to prices as the most urgent problem facing the country.

In February the first British soldier was killed in Belfast, to be followed by more military and civilian deaths as violence escalated. In the summer of 1970, three in five thought that the government had been right to send British troops to Northern Ireland, but this had dropped to two in five by June with almost as many thinking the government had been wrong. The problem of Ireland also jumped into third place the list of urgent problems, behind unemployment and prices. By September only a little over one in four approved of the government's handling of the situation in Northern Ireland, while almost twice as many disapproved. A month later, after British troops began to partially block unapproved roads to the border with the Republic, the figures were reversed. Although one in two approved of the action of troops, only half as many thought that it would succeed in cutting down the number of gunmen and arms' shipments entering Northern Ireland.

In mid-year a majority (three in five) still disapproved of the government applying for membership of the Common Market, though four in five felt that it was inevitable that Britain would eventually join. When asked what advantages there would be to Britain in becoming a member, one in three said that there were none, and the main advantage given, by one in five, was that British industry or agriculture would benefit. No other advantage reached double figures. On the other hand, only one in twenty said that there were no disadvantages, and two in three said that the cost of living and prices would go up. Manufacturers and financial people were thought to be the ones who would benefit if Britain joined, while pensioners, working people, housewives, farmers and fishermen would suffer. One bonus foreseen by the public was that British workers would enjoy more paid holidays, in line with the rest of Europe. Support for the government dropped through the first half of the year, losing 9 points between January and July. Support for Labour, on the other hand, rose by 8 points to 55 per cent in July, putting them at their all-time high since the war and a level they have rarely looked like achieving in the meantime.

In June 1971 the Russian three-man Soyuz II was successfully launched but the three cosmonauts were killed less than a month later during the landing. In late July the United States' Apollo 15 was launched, its astronauts landing on the Moon and returning safely in early August. These two events, naturally, increased the British public's feeling that the United States was ahead of Russia in space developments, and also had an effect on their attitudes towards flights in space. The public took the view that man should continue to go into space, but the Russian accident pushed up the 'machines only' group from fewer than one in three to two in five, a trend that was later reversed following the success of the Apollo mission.

In late October mainland China was elected to the United Nations and Taiwan lost her seat. On balance, people thought that it was wrong to expel Taiwan, but a little over one in two felt that China's admittance would be a good thing for the United Nations. It was also felt to make the UN more effective in keeping peace and that China would become friendlier to the United States, though it would have little effect on Chinese-Russian relations.

In December it was proposed that the Queen's income should be raised from about £500,000 to about £1 million a year. Although a majority felt that the government should give the Queen an increase, a majority also thought that the proposed increases were too high. At the same time people were asked whether or not MPs' salaries should be increased and a bare majority were opposed to the idea. One in two felt that an annual salary of £4500 plus expenses was too high for MPs, though two in five thought that it was about right. The Queen also emerged in the answers to a question on who was the most admired woman in the world, tying with Mrs Indira Gandhi, the Indian Prime Minister. The four most admired men were Harold Wilson, Prince Philip, Edward Heath and Ian Smith, the Rhodesian Prime Minister. The first three had also been the admired men of 1970. The public's choice as sports personality was George Best, the footballer, and another Royal, Princess Anne, as runner-up. The most popular film of 1971 was 'Soldier Blue', followed by 'The Sound of Music', a frequent favourite of the British public. 'Family at War', second in 1970, was the top television programme, with 'Coronation Street' in second place.

1972

The year started off rather badly, with a national miners' strike and 'Bloody Sunday' in Londonderry. In contrast with the miners' dispute in 1970, a majority of the public sided with the miners. In January unemployment topped the list of the most urgent problems, but by February that place had been taken by strikes. The public's sympathies, however, were still with the miners. On the question of Northern Ireland, the public disapproved, on balance, of the government's handling of the situation, though three in five felt that the government had been right to send troops to Northern Ireland. One in two also thought that the situation would get worse in the province if British troops were withdrawn. Three-quarters of the public felt that the government were right to blame the marchers and most of the blame for the Londonderry deaths was put on the marchers themselves or on the IRA. Less than one in ten blamed the soldiers.

When asked for the first time since the 1970 General Election who would win the next election, almost three in five of the public said that Labour would, while one in four favoured the Conservatives. On 18 February the Wilberforce Report on miners' pay was published. Four in five of the public felt that the Report was a fair one and two in three thought that the proposed increases were about right. On Mr Heath's handling of the miners' dispute, some might say a recurring event leading to his eventual downfall, the public said that their impression had declined. In April, however, Mr Heath's personal popularity was temporarily ahead of Mr Wilson's and Labour's lead was reduced to a mere 1 per cent, as Roy Jenkins and 7 other Labour MPs resigned from the Labour Front Bench. At the end of the month almost as many, two in five, felt that Mr Wilson should retire as thought he should carry on. Roy Jenkins was the public's choice as his possible successor, with Jim Callaghan a poor second. On the other hand, a British Rail work-to-rule, followed by a dock strike added to the government's industrial relations' problems. Almost three in five of the public at the time felt that there was a class struggle in Britain, an increase on the one in two found 8 years earlier.

On 23 June the pound was allowed to float and by mid-July Labour had gone into a 10-points lead. Two in five thought that the pound would have to devalue, but one in three felt that it could be avoided. The public's confusion over devaluation can be seen in the replies to a question on whether it would help to strengthen the economic position. Although, on balance, people felt that it would not, the biggest single answer, given by two in five, was that they did not know. Only one in three, however, thought that the government should resign if the pound had to be devalued. Reginald Maudling resigned as Home Secretary in mid-July, with a little over one in two of the public thinking he had been right to do so. One in three felt that his resignation would be a bad thing for the country as a whole, and one-half saw it as being bad for the Conservative party.

In Gallup's survey of attitudes towards the unions in the run-up to the 1972 Trades Union Congress, one in ten of the public said that the Industrial Relations Act, almost 2 years after its introduction, was the most urgent problem facing the unions. More, though, thought that strikes and unemployment were the urgent problems. A little over two in five approved of the government's Industrial Relations Act, though only one in four that the government would succeed in cutting down strikes,and one in two felt that the Act was harming industrial relations in the country. Two in five also felt that the Act should be suspended temporaily or repealed altogether. In the same survey people were almost evenly divided on whether the government should take compulsory powers to stop wages and other incomes from rising or rely on voluntary restraint by the unions, employers and others concerned.

The following month the government announced plans for a prices and incomes policy. By early October two in three of the public were aware of the government's proposals and a little over one in two approved of the limit on pay rises, while three in four approved of limiting shop price increases. Around one in two thought that the unions should accept the proposals, felt that they would help to solve the problem of inflation and that the plan would be a help to themselves and their family. Only one in three thought that the plan should be made compulsory, as it became on 6 November. The public's initial reaction to the latest of a series of prices and incomes policies over the years was better than that of similar policies in the mid-1960s. Around one in two thought that the policy was a good thing and felt that it was fair, though only one in four thought that it would be a success, and slightly more felt that the wage freeze would collapse than thought that the government would be able to maintain it.

As the year came to an end, with just a few weeks to go before Britain joined the European Economic Community, the British public remained anti-European, with more against membership than were for it. The balance of opinion was also that the agreement leading to Britain's membership was not the best that could be achieved and three in four disapproved of the government's proposal to spend £350,000 on a 'Festival of Europe'.

Three television programmes shared the most popular spot in 1972: 'Coronation Street', 'Upstairs Downstairs' and 'The Onedin Line'. This made the ninth time that 'Coronation Street' had topped the list. The most popular film of the year was 'The Godfather' - the first time such a film had headed the list - followed by 'Love Story' and 'Fiddler on the Roof'. Mark Spitz, the American Olympic swimmer, was the sports personality of the year, with athlete Mary Peters in second place and goalkeeper Gordon Banks third. The Queen and Prince Philip, in their Silver Wedding year, were the woman and man most admired by the public. The runners-up were Mrs Golda Meir in the female list, with President Nixon, Edward Heath and Enoch Powell in the men's.

1973

Even after joining the European Community, on 1 January, the public were still almost evenly divided on the decision, and one in three said that they would be pleased to hear that it had been scrapped. It was not a good start to the year either for Harold Wilson, his personal popularity dropping 10 points in 2 months, so that in January he was just 2 points ahead of Mr Heath. Neither was the public any more enthusiastic about the government's prices and incomes policy. On all the questions about the policy, the positive replies went down between the end of 1972 and January 1973. In spite of this, however, a majority of the public felt that the economic restrictions should continue, though two in three saw them as being stricter on wages than on prices.

In early January Gallup tested the Wilson-Patterson Conservatism Scale, where people were asked whether they favoured or believed in 50 different items, ranging from birth control, with which more than four in five were in favour, to suicide, which a little over one in ten believed in. Others of the 50 items were the death penalty (two in three favoured), school uniforms (three in five), moral training (four in five), nudist camps (one in three), Bible truth (one in two), white superiority (one in four), chastity (one in two) and church authority (two in five). A month later people were asked to judge how much influence various groups had on the country's future - a lot, a little or none at all. The most influential groups of the dozen groups surveyed were the Prime Minister and the trade unions, three in four thinking they each had a lot of influence. Next came big business, two in three saying they had a lot of influence, and cabinet ministers (a little over one in two). At the bottom of the list came 'people like yourself' with less than one in thirty thinking they had a lot of influence, while almost two in three felt they had none at all.

In a separate study on housekeeping allowances at about the same time, two in three married women said that they knew how much their husband's take-home pay was. Almost three in four said that they knew when their husband last had a pay rise but only 62 per cent knew how much rise he had been given. Two in three also thought that they had received a fair share of the rise for their housekeeping allowance, though 17 per cent thought otherwise. Greatest criticism came on whether their present housekeeping allowance was sufficient or not, 56 per cent saying it was not but among these, 37 per cent felt that their husband could not afford to increase it. A related topic was the public's attitude towards advertising, an industry which only one in four thought was a particularly important one for the country and which one in two felt too much money was spent on. Almost eight in ten (78 per cent) thought that advertising rendered a useful service in letting people know about new products, but almost as many (69 per cent) felt that it encouraged people to buy products they really did not want, and only 21 per cent felt that it helped to keep down the cost of living. On 1 April, an unfortunate piece of timing, Phase Two of the Prices and Incomes Policy came into being. In mid-April people were asked about the effect of VAT - recently introduced - on various products and services. The basic picture from the answers was that the government had succeeded in its attempts to explain the changes in press notices, but there was some confusion in the minds of the public on some of the items. One in four, for example, thought that the price of cars had gone up, whereas the effect of VAT should have been to bring them down in price.

In May Lord Lambton and Earl Jellicoe resigned from the government in circumstances reminiscent of the Profumo affair a decade before. The public, however, reacted quite differently to the two events: in 1963 a majority felt that the lives of cabinet ministers should be above reproach, but in 1973 the position was reversed and a majority said that they should be able to lead their lives as they wished. Similarly, in contrast to the earlier affair, people were less inclined to see any serious security risks involved or to see any serious effect on Britain's reputation abroad.

Also in May, for the first time, people in Britain were asked about the so-called 'Watergate' affair involving President Nixon of the United States. By then nine in ten were aware of the affair and 55 per cent of these thought that the President had not told the whole truth. One in two of those aware also thought that he knew in advance about the Watergate bugging and 56 per cent felt that he had participated in a cover-up. Naturally, a little over one in three said that their opinion of President Nixon had gone down, while only 2 per cent mentioned an improvement. A later study in mid-July found that 70 per cent of the British public thought that President Nixon had actually planned the bugging operation from the beginning, or did not plan it but knew about it in advance, or was an accessory after the fact. Only one in ten felt that he had no knowledge of the bugging and spoke up as soon as he had learnt about it.

In September, again for the first time, Gallup asked people how important a number of possible causes were to explain the increase in crime and violence in the country. Twelve possibilities were put forward and two of these were rated as 'very important' by six in ten - a general breakdown in respect for authority, law and order, and that laws were too lenient and did not let the police do their job. These were followed by bad examples set by parents and the use of drugs, mentioned by one in two as being a very important cause of crime and violence. At about the same time comparisons were made with a 1968 study on attitudes towards mixed marriages. Agreement with marriages between Catholics and Protestants had increased from 61 per cent in 1968 to 71 per cent, between Jews and non-Jews from 50 per cent to 61 per cent, and between whites and non-whites from 29 per cent to 45 per cent. Significant changes had also taken place since 1968 in the public's stereotypes of the Irish people, both north and south. From 1968 to 1973 the proportion thinking the people of Northern Ireland were intolerant rose from 8 per cent to 44 per cent, and insincere from 5 per cent to 19 per cent. On the other hand, an image of being hard-working fell from 34 per cent to 20 per cent and being friendly from 35 per cent to 14 per cent. Similarly, the public's image of the southern Irish had changed in the same direction, the main differences being in the final pattern of replies. The top two stereotypes for the people from north of the border were that they were intolerant and hard-working, while people from south of the border were thought to be poor yet friendly.

In the autumn of 1973, to celebrate 35 years of polling for newspapers, a variety of questions were repeated from the dark days of the late 1930s. Belief in life after death, visiting a dentist and participation in football pools, for example, had hardly changed. A little under one in four had visited a dentist in the previous six months. We still preferred to be inland rather than living by the seaside, though given a choice between the city and the country, we were more inclined to choose the latter, three in four doing so. We were slightly less likely in 1973 than in 1938 to have a pet but if we did we had more pets than 35 years previously. When asked in 1939 what the ideal number of children was for a family, 28 per cent said four or more but this had dropped to 15 per cent by 1973.

As the year came to an end the government's introduction of Phase III of its Prices and Incomes Policy did little to lessen the public's pessimism on the economic situation, particularly on prices, the precise issue which had won the 1970 General Election for Mr Heath. The policy as a whole was less acceptable to the public than it had been on the introduction of

Phases I and II. On 12 November the miners started an overtime ban, pushing public concern about strikes up from 5 per cent in October to 16 per cent in November and to 26 per cent in December. Also, by December, the fuel shortage topped the public's list of the most urgent problems facing the country. When asked who would win the next general election, the Conservatives and Labour in November were even with around one in three each, but by December Labour were the public's favourites to win.

From the beginning the public's sympathies were with the miners, though, as always, they disapproved of the miners' methods and thought that they were irresponsible. Initially they felt that the proposed increases for the miners were about right and three in four thought that the miners should not be taken as a special case outside the government's incomes policy. In mid-December ASLEF started to work-to-rule and a 3-day week was announced to save electricity.

Among the gloom, people were asked what was the best television programme they had seen in 1973. The four most popular were 'Crossroads', 'The Morecambe and Wise Show', 'Helen, a Woman of Today', and 'The Onedin Line'. 'Coronation Street', the previous long-running favourite, did not appear in the top six programmes. The most popular film of the year was the latest James Bond thriller, 'Live and Let Die', with 1972's winner 'The Godfather' in second place. The overwhelming choice as sports personality of the year was racing driver Jackie Stewart, with athlete Mary Peters second, as in 1972. Mrs Golda Meir, of Israel, possibly because of sympathies aroused during the Yom Kippur War, was the most admired woman, with the Queen in second place. There was no clear leader for the most admired man, with five sharing the top place: Edward Heath, Prince Philip, President Nixon, Enoch Powell and Dr Henry Kissinger.

1974

The year had hardly begun before there was intense speculation on an election in early February. The Conservatives held a slim 2-point lead over Labour, while Mr Heath's personal popularity was on a par with that of Mr Wilson, and the Conservatives had become the public's favourite to win the election. On the other hand, the public's attitude towards the miners was becoming more supportive, with a majority thinking that they should be taken as a special case outside the incomes policy and, on balance, thinking that the proposed increases were too low, despite the miners' decision to strike.

In the event, the Conservatives emerged with the largest share of the votes but with fewer seats than Labour, while the Liberals' share had

7 1974-1979: Labour Returns

The public's initial rating of Harold Wilson as Prime Minister was in contrast to Ted Heath's: in April 1974 53 per cent said that they were satisfied with Wilson, compared with an average of 37 per cent for Heath's premiership. In terms of party support, Labour started out with an 8-points' advantage over the Conservatives, increasing to 16 points by April. Economically, the average index of earnings was rising faster than the retail price index, with unemployment running around the 500,000 mark. The most urgent problems facing the new government were thought to be strikes and prices, each mentioned by around one in three of the public. Only one in three felt that Labour would succeed in solving the problems it faced.

As the year passed the public became less favourable to the government's prices and incomes policy, with majorities thinking that the policy was not fair to all concerned, and that they were not doing enough to control the rise in prices. With the settlement of the miners' strike in early March, the cost of living dominated the public's list of urgent problems, though Ireland got into second place. With the two-week strike and the resignation of the Northern Ireland Executive, a return to direct rule was confirmed. A little over one in two thought that the government was right to impose direct rule from Westminster, but two in three felt that the chances of the new moves bringing peace to Ireland were at best not very good. Again, a little over one in two thought that British troops should be withdrawn from Northern Ireland, though almost as many felt that such an action would make the situation worse and almost three in four thought that there was danger of civil war in the province.

Another election in 1974 was a foregone conclusion with the actual date being really the only thing in doubt. In June a majority of the public thought that the government should carry on but by July the majority view was for an election in the near future. When asked in August who was mainly to blame for Britain's economic difficulties, 10 per cent blamed Labour, 26 per cent blamed the previous Conservative administration and 38 per cent blamed them both. On 18 September the election was announced and Labour went into the campaign with a 5 points lead over the Conservatives, very similar to the 3.6 per cent win they achieved on election day itself.

In contrast to the February election, people were less interested in who would win in October, and whereas in February a majority had expected the Conservatives to win, Labour were the public's guess in October. The cost of living remained the country's most urgent problem in the public's view and Labour was thought the best party to handle the problem. Mr Heath emerged from the two 1974 elections with a decidedly battered image. Among those people who had seen him on television, the feeling was that his appearances had not helped his party. In a poll in late October, one in two felt that some other person should take over as leader of the Conservative party and the public's choice was Mr William Whitelaw. In a two-way run-off against Mr Whitelaw, Mr Powell, Mrs Thatcher and Sir Keith Joseph, Mr Heath was thought to be a better leader than either Mr Powell or Mrs Thatcher, worse than Mr Whitelaw and about on par with Sir Keith. Discussions about a change in the leadership led to almost two in three of the public thinking that the Conservatives were a divided party.

The year ended with Gallup's round-up of the public's choices of admired personalities, films and television programmes. Dr Henry Kissinger and Harold Wilson were the two most admired men, with the Queen dominating the list of admired women, followed by Mrs Golda Meir and Mrs Indira Gandhi. For the second year running 'Crossroads' was the most popular television programme of the year, with 'Upstairs, Downstairs' and 'The Brothers' sharing second place. The most popular item on the silver screen was 'The Sting' with 'The Exorcist' as runner-up. The overwhelming choice as the sports personality of the year was the world champion boxer Muhammed Ali (ex Cassius Clay), with another boxer, John Conteh, in second place.

1975

January found the Conservatives 14.5 points behind Labour, with Mr Heath's personal rating at its lowest level since June 1970. On 11 February Margaret Thatcher was elected Conservative leader and the political scene was transformed. The Conservatives went ahead of Labour by 4 points in February and, in contrast to earlier studies, two in three felt that Mrs Thatcher would prove to be a good leader. Almost three in four of the public took the view that Mr Heath was right to have resigned and that the changeover helped to heal the public's image of a divided Conservative party. As in the past, the party's choice of leader was not the public's. When asked in January who should take over from Mr Heath if he resigned, the public's spontaneous favourite was Mr Whitelaw, followed by Sir Keith Joseph, with Mrs Thatcher in third place. The order was still the same when the public was prompted with a number of possibilities: Mrs Thatcher obtaining around one-third of the votes awarded to Mr Whitelaw. The year was also to be remembered for the first nationwide referendum in Britain, on the continued membership of the European Common Market. Much time had been spent in discussions about renegotiating Britain's membership and on 23 January the government's first statement was made on the referendum procedure. Early surveys showed that although people felt that we had been wrong to join the European Community in the first place, a majority would vote to stay in.

In February Gallup asked people if they knew the imperial equivalent of various metric measurements - to bring us in line with the rest of Europe. The results were not particularly good, either from a viewpoint of British educational standards or Europeanisation. Only one in two knew roughly what the British equivalent of a metre and a litre were, and a little over one in three got close to the answer on a kilometre and a kilo. When asked whether they approved or disapproved of a switch-over to the metric system, one in three supported the move but one in two were opposed. From March onwards, up to the vote on 5 June, a number of surveys dealt in detail with British attitudes towards the Common Market and the possible effects of being either a member or a non-menber. These tended to show that one of the most important issues was the Market's impact on prices in Britain and that this was a negative item. On the positive side were military or defence links with Europe but this was rated relatively low in importance compared with other issues. On the other hand, one in two felt that leaving the Common Market would weaken the British economy. In political terms, the public was confused to some degree on where the parties stood on Britain's membership. The vast majority, four in five, for example, knew that the Conservatives wanted Britain to remain a member; but whereas one in three thought Labour wanted to stay in, another one in three saw the party as undecided. There can be little doubt that the issue contributed to the public's view of Labour as a divided party - three in four shared this view - and it was also unfortunate for the anti-Marketeers that their main speakers in the Labour ranks had a negative appeal to the electorate. As far as the Liberal party was concerned, two in five were uncertain of their policy, but the tendency was to see them as pro-Market.

With Britain's membership, British Gallup joined her European colleagues in the biannual 'Eurobarometer' series of studies conducted for the Commission of the European Communities. The bulk of these surveys deal with changing attitudes towards the Community itself and its institutions, but periodically tackle other issues in some depth. In May, for example, a survey was conducted across the nine countries of the Community to mark International Women's Year. Questions covered the status of women, the roles of the sexes, social reforms, personal satisfaction and happiness, and attitudes towards Europe. The resulting report, published in December 1975 ran to over 200 pages of detailed analysis, only part of which we have space for here. For example, whereas 20 per cent of the British could be said to attach a high degree of importance to the situation of women in society, the proportion was 32 per cent for the Community as a whole and only the Netherlands rated it as less important. Similarly, when asked whether they felt that the majority of women wanted fewer differences between the roles of the sexes in society, 64 per cent thought they did compared with 73 per cent overall. Again only one country, this time Denmark, scored lower on the question. Should politics be left to men? Across the European Community, 36 per cent of men and 34 per cent of women agreed with this concept, but in the United Kingdom the figures were 26 per cent and 25 per cent respectively. We also had a significantly higher proportion than the Community average thinking that men and women should play the same role in politics.

In May questions were asked for the first time dealing with the public's trust in other countries and the degree to which they wanted to be involved in helping certain countries if they were invaded. Naturally, almost one in two of the British public felt that they could trust the United States 'a great deal' as an ally in case of war. One in three had the same level of trust in Norway and in Denmark, one in four trusted West Germany 'a great deal' and one in six France. When it came to a question on the reciprocal arrangement - what Britain should do if a country were to be invaded by communist-backed forces - we were most prepared to send troops to Australia and Canada (one in two favoured this option). Around one in three favoured sending troops in defence of the United States, and one in four for defending West Germany.

Two months later people were asked which countries produced goods of high quality, a question first asked in 1960. The replies showed a dramatic shift in attitudes towards foreign goods. In 1960, for example, the United States dominated the table with 62 per cent thinking she produced high quality goods. Fifteen years later she had slumped to just 25 per cent, putting her in tenth position. West Germany, third in 1960, moved to the top, while Japan who were twenty-third in the 1960 table rose to take the number two spot. Australia, New Zealand and Switzerland took the remaining top positions in both studies, though with significantly fewer people in 1975 picking their products as being of a high quality.

In July Mr Wilson announced Phase I of his pay policy, at a time when the annual rate of inflation was in excess of 25 per cent. Three in four saw inflation as the most urgent problem facing the country at the time, and almost as many (71 per cent) thought that the government should take compulsory powers to stop wages and other incomes from rising too fast. Three in four also felt that the government had not handled wage claims firmly enough and approved of their policy of trying to restrict wage claims as much as possible. On the other hand, almost two in three thought that the trade unions were taking an unreasonable attitude towards the government's prices and incomes policy, and one in two felt that the unions were mainly to blame for Britain's rising prices, while just over one in three also blamed the unions and their wage claims for the rise in unemployment. When asked what had been the biggest failures of the government, the top three were failure to keep down prices (68 per cent), failure to stop wages rising too fast (58 per cent) and failure to stop strikes (54 per cent). Given these findings it was of little surprise that only one in four of the public thought that the salaries of Members of Parliament should be increased, and that a little over one in two felt that Labour had not kept their election promises.

Another measure of Britain's relative decline in a changing world can be found in the results to a question in September on which country produced the best motor cars. In 1960 three in four of the British public said that the best cars were home-produced, but fifteen years later only one in three did so, with Germany and Japan providing strong competition. Of perhaps only historical or educational interest are the results to a question in October on the public's knowledge of various dates in history. While two in three, for example, correctly identified 1066 with the Battle of Hastings, only 16 per cent associated the Magna Carta with 1215, 10 per cent associated Columbus with 1492, while even fewer, 5 per cent, associated the Declaration of Independence with 1776.

In late November, following Franco's death, the British public were asked to say how history would remember him. More than four in five, as in 1970 with de Gaulle, felt that his name would go down in history. The contrast, however, was that the public felt that Franco would be remembered unfavourably, while de Gaulle would be remembered favourably. Majorities thought that Spain would become more democratic following Franco's death, that her relations with the rest of the world would improve and that she should be allowed to join the Common Market.

Mention has been made earlier of the study conducted in May across the European Community to mark International Women's Year. During October and November a similar study was conducted but this time on the topic of 'European Consumers', covering such things as finances, advertising, consumer information and product tests. Questions were asked, for example, on how people would react to rising prices: shop around, put off expenditure, look for sales etc. Across eleven such activities, the British were less active than the Community overall, particularly on the idea of getting together with other consumers. Only the Danes were significantly less enthusiastic on this point. Almost one in two (47 per cent) of the British claimed to have been cheated over a purchase in the recent past, second only to Italy (53 per cent) in the Community table. The United Kingdom also came second to Italy on a question on having to complain about public services: 60 per cent in Italy and 41 per cent in the UK. Although the British were less likely to give attention to the unit price when shopping than were the Community as a whole, we were more likely to give attention to the amount weighed. Thirteen per cent, however, confessed to never checking the bill. When it came to whether people had sufficient information, the UK came sixth out of the nine countries as far as shopping for major items was concerned and seventh for shopping for food. On advertising, 57 per cent of the British agreed that it provided consumers with useful information, but 78 per cent thought that it often made consumers buy goods they did not really need and the same proportion felt that advertising often misled consumers on product quality. On the other hand, public awareness of specialised consumer information publications or press articles was highest in the UK, with two in five claiming knowledge of specialised publications, and one in two were aware of consumer protection organisations and product comparison tests.

With perhaps more than a touch of irony, the public at the end of 1975 named Mrs Thatcher as their most admired woman and Mr Heath as their most admired man. Mrs Thatcher narrowly squeezed the Queen into second place, with Mrs Gandhi third; behind Mr Heath came Dr Henry Kissinger and Prince Charles.

1976

The year began with Labour narrowly in the lead by 1.5 per cent over the Conservatives, Mr Wilson and Mrs Thatcher level in terms of personal popularity. The cost of living remained in the public's view as the most urgent problem facing the country, mentioned by one in two of those asked. On balance the government's prices and incomes policy was thought to be a good thing, the public still approved of their policy of trying to restrict wage claims as much as possible, but felt that not enough was being done to control the rise in prices. The effect on the public was evident from the six in ten who said that they were worse off compared with a year before, and from the four in ten who thought that they would be worse off in a year's time.

In mid-March, for the first time, people were asked about the Conservative party's attitudes towards trade unions. Then, the public was almost evenly divided with around four in ten each thinking that the party was hostile to the unions or not hostile. On balance people felt that relations between the two would improve in the future. On 16 March Harold Wilson resigned and was succeeded by James Callaghan on 5 April. A little over a month later, on 10 May, Jeremy Thorpe resigned as Liberal leader, his place being taken by David Steel on 7 July. The public's initial reaction to Mr Callaghan was favourable: 57 per cent expressing satisfaction with him, and Labour took a 5.5 per cent lead over the Conservatives, compared with a 2.5 per cent Tory advantage in March. Mr Healey's Budget for 1976 was also well-received, and proved not only to be his most popular but also one of the four most popular since the war. Despite the increased party support for Labour, however, the public's reaction to Mr Wilson's resignation was one of sorrow, which they viewed as leading to a weaker, more divided party.

In May Gallup asked two questions about the future of nuclear energy in Britain. Then, four in ten of the public thought that nuclear power generation should be increased, two in ten felt that no more should be developed and around one in seven wanted it stopped completely. When asked what they would do if a nuclear power station were to be built in their area, one in five said that they would agree to it, one in four said that they would not oppose it though they would feel anxious about it, one in three said they would oppose it, and the remainder were either undecided or unconcerned.

Mr Steel's entry into the political arena as a party leader was fairly well-received with 45 per cent thinking that he would prove a good leader for the Liberals and 11 per cent taking the opposite view. Support for the Liberals rose to 13 per cent in July, just one point below their highest for the year. The following month questions were asked to measure satisfaction with the political system. The public were evenly divided on whether or not the then present parliamentary system was satisfactory or not, but they differed in their strength of feeling: the opponents of the system were much stronger in their convictions than the supporters were.

With the announcement on 9 September that unemployment had passed the 1.5 million mark, one in four mentioned it as the most urgent problem facing the country, though it still remained firmly in second place behind the cost of living and in fact fell back in October. In answer to another question, forcing people to choose between trying to curb inflation or trying to reduce unemployment, a little over one in two opted for a policy on inflation, while just over one in three wanted to fight unemployment.

Two in three felt that the government was not doing enough to stop the rise in unemployment, though two in three workers felt that their jobs were safe. By October the Conservatives had taken a lead of 11.5 per cent and then more than doubled to a 25-points advantage in November. Their level of support at 55 per cent proved to be only the second highest for the party since the war. To make matters worse for Labour, two in three of the public thought that the government's views were not representative of the public as a whole, and the public was also becoming increasingly disenchanted with the prices and incomes policy.

In December a study for BBC TV's 'Man Alive' programme not only interviewed the general public, but also a sample of managers and directors in business, on the economy. While three in four of the public viewed Britain's economic problems as very serious, almost nine in ten of the professionals did so. The two groups were also in agreement as to who was mainly to blame for these problems: the trade unions, followed by politicians. Three in four workers and two in three of the professionals felt that they, personally, were working as hard as they should, but around two in three felt that the people they knew were, and less than one in five thought that British workers in general worked as hard as they should. Similarly, only one in four of the public and one in three professionals thought that British management pulled its weight. The question that perhaps aroused the most interest dealt with which of four people - Jack Jones, Jim Callaghan, Mrs Thatcher and John Methven - had the most power and influence in the country. More than one in two of the public and almost two in three professionals named Jack Jones as the most influential, with Mr Callaghan a poor second. On the other hand, majorities expressed dissatisfaction with the way Mr Jones used his influence.

Mrs Thatcher again ended the year, as in 1975, as the public's most admired woman, closely followed by the Queen, also second the previous year. Dr Henry Kissinger, the American Secretary of State, second in 1975, was the most admired man of the year, with Mr Heath and Prince Charles in second and third places. The top three men, therefore, in 1975 also became the top three in 1976, though their relative postions had changed.

1977

The year began with three in four of the public believing that food prices had gone up a great deal, while a little over one in two felt that wages had risen either very little or not at all. More than four in five also felt that food prices had gone up more than wages. The average amount spent on food was £18 per week, and the 'ideal' income for a family of four was thought to be £62 per week. When asked in February about an enlarged Common Market, around four in ten were in favour of allowing Spain, Portugal and Greece to join. At the same time, one in three of the public - including one in two under 25s - wanted to emigrate, with Canada, Australia and New Zealand as the top three new homelands. Around six in ten of the people who wanted to emigrate, however, felt that it was something they would like to do but could not see happening. Better opportunities and having family or friends in other countries were the two main reasons given by people wanting to emigrate.

In March the spotlight turned to Concorde, an Anglo-French achievement of which two in three said that they were proud. One in three, however, thought that Concorde would damage the environment, though one in two thought that it would not. The public were naturally hostile to the attempts by some American groups to prevent British Airways' Concordes landing in New York, and approved on balance of counter-restrictions.

Also in March, on the 23rd, the Lib-Lab pact saved the government in a vote of confidence and for the first time since 1931 Britain had a government explicitly dependent on an understanding with a party not in government. The irony of the situation was that whatever power or influence the Liberals may have had with the Labour government was counter-productive in terms of party support. Starting at 14.5 per cent in January, their support dropped to 8 per cent later in the year, their lowest point since the 1974 election. In May, not unnaturally, one in two of the public felt that the pact was a good thing for the government, but bad for both the Liberals and the Conservatives, and was, on balance, bad for the country as a whole. Three in four felt that the Liberals had little or no influence on the government's policies and a little over one in two thought that the Liberals would suffer at the next election by a decline in their vote. Mr Steel's personal popularity touched a low point in May with only one in three thinking that he was proving a good leader.

Questions originally asked in the early 1950s were repeated in May 1977 to see what degree attitudes and opinions had changed in the intervening 25 years. The 'ideal' number of children in a family, for example, had dropped from 3 to 2.4. The earliest age at which boys and girls should be allowed to marry had also fallen, from an average 22 for boys to 21, and from 21 for girls to 19. The public at that point of time in 1977 professed to be happier than the public had been in 1952: 55 per cent saying that they were very happy compared with 41 per cent twenty years before. The greatest change was in how the parties were viewed. In 1952 59 per cent thought that there were real important differences between the parties but by 1977 the figure had dropped to 34 per cent. A further question in August, asked earlier in 1958, showed how the public's attitude towards artificial insemination had changed: in 1958 two in ten approved and one in two disapproved, but in 1977 the figures had reversed.

By July the public were taking a more favourable view of the Lib-Lab pact. Majorities still felt that it was good for the government and bad for the Conservatives, but were more evenly balanced on its effect on the country and on the Liberals. This was also reflected in the public's perception of how much influence the Liberals had on government policies: 19 per cent in May said that it was at least considerable, rising to 34 per cent in July. In August people on balance said that they would be less inclined to support the Liberal party if they pulled out of the pact.

Again in August, questions were asked about homosexuals. One was a repeat from 1957, when 19 per cent of men said that they had at some time in their life been approached by a homosexual, rising to 24 per cent in 1977. Majorities of the public felt that homosexuals should be hired as sales staff or for the armed forces, but majorities were opposed to them becoming junior school teachers, doctors or prison officers. Two in five felt that there were more homosexuals than there had been 25 years earlier, though one in four thought not. The public were mixed in their views as to the cause of homosexuality: one in three said that it was something a person was born with, one in four said that it was due to upbringing or environment, while one in five thought it was a mixture of the two. Almost three in five felt that homosexual relations between consenting adults should be legal.

On 13 August a National Front march led to clashes in Lewisham and nine in ten of the public said that they were aware of the violence that had accompanied the marches. When asked who was mainly to blame for the violence, the public was evenly divided between the National Front and their opponents: just under one in two thought the marches should be banned but slightly fewer, two in five, took the opposite view.

The year ended with Labour a single half-point ahead of the Conservatives, with the Liberals at their lowest level since the 1974 election. There were now three urgent problems facing the country, as far as the public were concerned: inflation (32 per cent), unemployment (23 per cent) and strikes (19 per cent). Two in three of the public said that they would approve if the police and firemen (then on strike) received pay rises in excess of the government's pay guidelines, but majorities said that they would disapprove if miners, merchant seamen, railwaymen, local authority manual workers and power station workers were to do so. Majority approval emerged in another study for nurses and doctors to be treated as a special case, but not for postmen, water and sewage workers or dockers.

1978

In January Mrs Thatcher commented on television that 'people can feel rather swamped' by immigration, at a time when two in three of the public felt that there should be restrictions on the entry of coloured people from the Commonwealth and more than two in ten thought that they should be kept out completely. Even before the statement, one in two of the public were aware of the Conservative party policy on immigration and more than seven in ten of this group knew that it proposed restrictions and approved of the policy. A month later, majorities agreed that Britain was in danger of being swamped, that the social services and NHS would suffer if there were not as many coloured doctors and coloured nurses, and that Labour was not controlling coloured immigration, but majorities disagreed with the idea of letting in just white immigrants, and that there was little that could be done about reducing immigration. Around two in ten mentioned immigrants in February and March as one of the two most urgent problems facing the country, but the proportion slowly subsided so that it was down to one in ten within a few months. At the same time, unemployment took over from inflation as the most urgent problem. Mr Healey's Budget, with 68 per cent thinking it a fair one, was the most popular in almost thirty years of questioning and that level has still to be surpassed.

In May people were asked whether they felt that they had enough say in how various things in society were organised. Only 15 per cent, for example, thought that they had enough say in the services provided by the nationalised industries, and similar proportions took the same view of the way local authorities worked, the TV programmes put out by the BBC and the commercial companies, and the way the government ran the country. Around one in four thought that they had enough say in the policies pursued by employers, trade union policies, the education system, the running of banks and building societies, and the way newspapers presented the news. People were most contented with their influence on their working conditions (36 per cent) and the services provided by shops (41 per cent).

People were also asked in May to rate six countries - Russia, the United States, Italy, France, Japan and West Germany - on an eleven-point capitalist/socialist scale and separately on an eleven-point non-verbal favourability scale, ranging from +5 to - 5. In addition, Britain was rated on the capitalist/socialist scale and scored an average of 4.2, where 0 meant a country was thought to be completely capitalist and 10 completely socialist. As in politics, therefore, Britain was rated slightly to the right of centre. This compared with an average of 8.1 for Russia, seen as the most socialist of the seven countries, and 2.8 for the United States, seen as the most capitalist. In between these two extremes were West Germany (4.0), Japan (4.6), France (4.8) and Italy (5.7). The United States scored highest on the favourability scale with an average of +1.9 out of a maximum of +5, closely followed by West Germany (+1.6), France (+0.8), Japan (+0.4), Italy (+0.1) and Russia at the bottom with -1.9, against a possible low of -5.

As the year progressed, the proportion of the public wanting a general election in the near future increased, from 40 per cent in January to an absolute majority of 54 per cent in June. Support for the two main parties was dead level at 45.5 per cent, with the Liberals at a low of 6 per cent. When asked who they expected to win an election, the public were similarly divided: slightly more thinking Labour would win than mentioned the Conservatives. In July, when asked to envisage a Labour victory, majorities thought that this would mean more government help for the nationalised industries and, on balance, more union power, more control of incomes, more direct taxation, more unemployment, more government control over peoples' lives, more inflation and less encouragement for small businesses. On the other hand, a Conservative victory was expected to lead to more encouragement for small businesses, fewer immigrants, less government help for the nationalised industries, less union power, less direct taxation and less control of incomes. When it came to policies they wanted a future government to follow, majorities of the public were in favour of limits on wage and price increases, doing more to reduce unemployment, tighter immigration controls, longer prison sentences, not paying social security benefits to the families of strikers, improving the NHS, selling council homes to their tenants, allowing the retention of grammar schools, increasing pensions and withdrawing British troops from Northern Ireland. Majorities were against giving unions seats on the boards of major companies, nationalising more industries and abolishing the House of Lords.

In October people were asked how they viewed some general changes that had been taking place in Britain - whether things had gone too far or not far enough. Seven in ten, for example, felt that people showing less respect for authority had gone too far, and almost six in ten shared the same view about moves to go easier on people who broke the law and the right to show nudity and sex in films or magazines - they had gone too far. A little over one in two also thought that the reduction of Britain's military strength had gone too far.

1979

Election year opened with the Conservatives 7.5 points ahead of Labour, with the Liberals nowhere at only 6 per cent support across the country. Almost one in two of the public were satisfied with Mr Callaghan as Prime Minister, a higher personal rating than for either Mrs Thatcher or Mr Steel as leaders of their respective parties. Almost two in three wanted an election and the public felt the Conservatives would win. A little over one in two said that strikes were the most urgent problem facing the country, up from only one in ten in December. Mr Callaghan's apparent lack of concern over the situation on his return from Guadaloupe in mid-January pushed his personal rating down 15 points in just a month, and saw the Conservatives take a 20-points lead over Labour. Just one in ten approved of the way the government was handling strikes and labour relations, while more than eight in ten disapproved. One in two of the public felt that the situation was serious enough to declare a state of emergency.

A study at the same time but confined to Scotland asked a number of questions about the referendum on a directly elected assembly. As in the nation as a whole, inflation and unemployment were the two topics electors wanted discussed at the coming general election chosen by around three in four Scots, while only two in ten chose independence as a topic. Interest in Scotland in the referendum was relatively low, with around one in three saying that they were very interested, another one in three were moderately interested and the remainder either expressed only a little interest or no interest at all. One in three wanted to stick with the current system of governing Scotland, while at the other extreme 14 per cent wanted an independent Scotland with a Scottish Parliament. Given these figures it is not surprising that the 'yes' vote failed to produce the required 40 per cent.

In April, as part of the biannual Eurobarometer series, British Gallup were involved in a study on Europeans and their children. It showed, for example, that among recipients of child benefits, 82 per cent in the UK felt that the allowances were vital or very useful for making ends meet, compared with 53 per cent across the Community. Not surprising, 'money' topped the list, in all countries, of problems experienced in raising children. Seven in ten UK parents felt that parents as a whole did not spend enough time with their children, and more (86 per cent) felt that the introduction of 'flexitime' would help them look after their children better. Only French parents were more enthusiastic about flexitime's potential. When it came to some positive attitudes to parenthood, the British were close to the bottom of the European league table. Asked whether they agreed or disagreed with two statements, 56 per cent agreed that 'to bring a child into the world shows faith in the future' and 53 per cent agreed that 'parenthood is the ultimate fulfilment of men and women'. Only the Danes and the Dutch, on the first of the statements, scored lower than the British. On the other hand, the UK, with 78 per cent, topped the table for the number of people thinking that present-day parents were not strict enough with their children and 63 per cent thought that parents were too indulgent towards their children. Almost one in two of the British public thought that parents were not concerned enough with their children's opinions and around one in two agreed that modern-day children were not taken sufficiently into account. Even more, six in ten, felt that parents were less close to their children than when they themselves had been children, suggesting a perceived widening in the gap between British parents and their offspring.

A question on the ideal number of children for a family in Britain in 1979 produced an average of 2.27 children compared with a range of 1.95 in West Germany and 3.62 in the Republic of Ireland. Two in three rejected the idea that 'the future of society is too uncertain to risk bringing children into the world'. None of the other countries involved in the study took such a strong stand against the concept. Two in three agreed that 'it's a pity that children do not have as much contact with their grandparents as they used to'. Only in France and in Luxembourg was agreement higher, with the Dutch the least likely to agree with the statement.

Among Gallup's final election survey data are a number of intriguing findings that contrast with the actual Conservative victory on polling day. Labour, for example, was ahead of the Conservatives as the party with the better leaders, was ahead on which party was 'best for people like yourself' and level with the Conservatives on which party had the best policies. On the other hand, the Conservatives had a narrow lead on which party could best handle the country's most urgent problems. It is perhaps a sad reflection on British politics that around four in ten Conservatives and one in three Labour supporters voted for negative reasons - their dislike of the other parties - than for something that they liked about their own party.

8 1979-1987: A New Conservative Philosophy

The 1979 general election put Mrs Thatcher into power, a position she still held 8 years later when this book was in the latter stages of being written. The public's initial reaction towards Mrs Thatcher as Prime Minister was mixed, with 41 per cent expressing satisfaction with her and 40 per cent expressing dissatisfaction. On the other hand, despite his defeat in the election, almost two in three (63 per cent) of the public felt that Mr Callaghan was proving a good leader of the Labour party. The cost of living was thought to be the most urgent problem facing the country in June, mentioned by 45 per cent, followed by unemployment (19 per cent). Sir Geoffrey Howe's first Budget was seen as a lack-lustre one compared with Mr Healey's in 1978, summarised in Gallup's article in The *Daily Telegraph* of 22 June as 'one of the least popular Budgets proposed by one of the least popular Chancellors in the last 27 years'. British electors returned to the polling booths in July as the first elections took place across the European Economic Community. As a measure of antipathy towards Europe, only one in three of the British public bothered to vote, compared with three in four in the preceding general election. Similarly, just one in two had been aware of the publicity campaign about the European elections.

By the time of the annual party conferences, the public's impression of both Mrs Thatcher and the Conservative party had gone down. Mrs Thatcher's supporters spoke of her positive, courageous personality, making an effort to get to grips with the country's problems. On the other hand, her detractors were concerned with her breaking her word and with her handling of the issues of the day, particularly inflation. Majorities of the public also felt that the goverment did too much for the well-to-do (61 per cent), but not enough for the working class (63 per cent) or for people living on small pensions or incomes (70 per cent). In November, when asked whether they agreed or disagreed with various statements about the government's taxation policy, majorities agreed with the statements 'the rich get richer, the poor get poorer' (71 per cent), 'not fair to the lower paid' (59 per cent) and 'people who want to work will gain' (50 per cent). On the other hand, substantial disagreement was found with the statements 'they are giving people the incentive to work harder' (53 per cent) and 'they try to give you the money you have earned' (50 per cent). At the same time, the average weekly amount spent on food had risen to £25 and the 'ideal income' for a family of four was thought to be £90 per week.

1980

The year 1980 opened with Labour 9 points in the lead over the Conservatives and Mrs Thatcher's personal popularity continuing to decline. The most urgent problems facing the country were thought to be the cost of living (30 per cent), strikes (24 per cent) and unemployment (15 per cent). The Russian invasion of Afghanistan on Christmas Day 1979 inevitably intruded into a supposedly non-political international event - the Moscow Olympic Games. In a study conducted in late January the vast majority (96 per cent) of the British public were aware of the possibility of some countries boycotting the Games and three in four of these knew that it was a consequence of Russia's modern-day return to Afghanistan. When asked whether Britain should withdraw from the Games, the public were almost evenly divided, with 41 per cent in favour and 44 per cent against. On 24 January plans were announced to site American cruise nuclear missiles in Britain. A Gallup study conducted around 10 days earlier found majorities of the public thinking that the Warsaw Pact countries had the strongest military forces (59 per cent) and were strongest in nuclear weapons (50 per cent). Only 13 per cent and 15 per cent respectively thought that NATO was the strongest. In terms of what was best for Britain's security, 67 per cent thought that we should have nuclear weapons. This was hardly surprising, given that in a separate survey at the end of the month 85 per cent of the public saw Russia as a military threat to Britain and to the rest of Europe. At the same time, around six in ten thought that there was much danger of world war, compared with only one in seven in mid 1975. The public had also become more belligerent: 60 per cent being willing to send troops to Australia, for example, if she were attacked by communist-backed forces, 57 per cent to Canada, 48 per cent to the United States and 41 per cent to West Germany. In 1976 the figures had been 51 per cent, 49 per cent, 33 per cent and 28 per cent respectively.

Despite these concerns about the international situation, the British had become decidedly less European-minded since 1975 when they had voted to remain a Community member. Majorities, for example, thought that it would be better for Britain to leave the Common Market for 'the price we pay for food' (68 per cent), 'the price we pay for other goods' (55 per cent) and 'Britain's relationship with the Commonwealth' (54 per cent). In 1975 the figures had only been around one-half of the 1980 figures. Similarly, 56 per cent felt that the British economy would be stronger out of the Common Market, whereas 51 per cent in 1975 thought that the economy would benefit by being in. Thus, 57 per cent thought that Britain's membership was a bad thing and 59 per cent, given the opportunity, would vote to leave the Community.

Of perhaps only marginal importance in Britain, but of greater importance in some other countries, was the cultural question of the sex of a child. In March 1980 a few questions were asked for BBC TV. Given the choice, people opted for a boy as their first child rather than a girl, by a margin of two to one, though almost one in two gave no preference. When it came to the sex of a second child, the figures were almost reversed. Eight in ten people were happy, however, to leave the matter to chance and only one in eight were interested in the possibility of choosing the sex of a child before birth.

As the level of unemployment rose throughout 1980, passing 1.5 million in April and 2 million in August, so the proportion seeing unemployment as the most urgent problem facing the country increased: from 23 per cent in May, to 29 per cent in June and to 49 per cent in July, toppling inflation from the top of the table. The four main reasons for the high level of unemployment were thought to be world economic pressures (35 per cent), the unions (25 per cent), the government (23 per cent) and people not wanting to work (23 per cent). Two in three people thought that the country was in 'deep and serious trouble'.

On 15 October Mr Callaghan retired as Labour leader, with Denis Healey and Mrs Shirley Williams the public's favourites for the position. Michael Foot was in fifth place. When asked who they would not like to see leading the Labour party, Tony Benn and Michael Foot dominated the replies. In the event, Michael Foot was elected leader and the public's initial reaction to him was not good. As many thought that he would not prove a good leader as thought he would - 38 per cent each. His personal rating never improved on this rather lowly level in the 3 years of his leadership, ending in September 1983, when it was obvious that his days were numbered, with only 9 per cent thinking that he was proving or had proved a good leader. Despite this antipathy towards Michael Foot, Labour ended 1980 12.5 per cent ahead of the Conservatives. Across the Atlantic on 4 November ex-actor Ronald Reagan defeated Jimmy Carter to become the new President of the United States. In contrast to the position 4 years earlier, when Mr Carter had been elected, the British public thought that, on balance, Mr Reagan's election would be good for America's relations with Britain but would be bad for America, bad for peace in the world and neither good nor bad for America's standing in the world.

1981

On 22 January Gallup's first survey of 1981 showed Labour still comfortably in the lead. Two days later a special conference of the party approved an electoral college for leadership elections, followed the next day by the announcement of the Council for Social Democracy, and the Social Democratic party was launched on 26 March, with Mrs Shirley Williams, Roy Jenkins, David Owen and Bill Rodgers as the so-called 'gang of four'. Labour's lead of 13.5 points rapidly evaporated, dropping to 7.5 points following the conference, and by mid-February the Conservatives had taken a slim half point-lead, with the Liberals standing at their highest point since the 1979 election. When asked in mid-February how they would vote given the choice of four parties, 21 per cent said that they would vote for the new SDP and 36 per cent said that they would support a Liberal/Social Democratic alliance - almost as many as for the Conservative and Labour parties combined. The following month, a week before the party had actually been launched, the SDP had a 14 per cent share of the vote, putting them, in combination with the Liberals, 2 per cent ahead of the Conservatives and 2 per cent behind Labour. Sir Geoffrey Howe's Budget for 1981 was even less well-received than his 1980 Budget, making it the least popular Budget proposed by the least popular Chancellor since the war.

On the wider, international scene, the public were also unhappy about Britain's position in the world: a growing proportion wanted Britain to try to be more like Sweden and Switzerland (57 per cent) than try to be a leading world power (29 per cent), with six in ten thinking that Britain's influence in the world had declined anyway. Even more, two in three, thought that Britain was moving away from prosperity - only one in four took this view in 1978 - and four in ten thought that Britain's prospects in the future were likely to get worse. The public were also changing their views of their allies. More were prepared to trust the USA 'a great deal' in case of war (62 per cent) than had been prepared to do so in 1975 (45 per cent). At the same time, trust in West Germany improved, while distrust of France increased.

April was marked by unemployment reaching 2.5 millions, accompanied by destructive riots in Brixton. In surveys of the most urgent problems facing the country, unemployment was consistently being mentioned as the number one problem by more than seven in ten of the general public. For the first time since the 1979 election, people were asked whether they agreed or disagreed with a number of statements about Mrs Thatcher. On the positive side, 91 per cent agreed that she was a strong personality, 85 per cent that she spoke her mind, 81 per cent that she was trying hard in her job, 80 per cent that she was a good speaker and 55 per cent that she knew what she was talking about. The public, however, were also highly critical: 73 per cent thought that she was not in touch with ordinary people, 53 per cent that she talked a lot but did little, 70 per cent that she was divisive, 57 per cent that her ideas were destructive, 67 per cent that she was self-centred and 51 per cent that she did not know about the problems of the cost of living.

In a follow up to the riots, Gallup asked people which of a number of issues they thought were serious social problems in Britain. Top of the list were crimes of violence (83 per cent), followed by juvenile crime (71 per cent), drug taking (63 per cent) and bad housing (58 per cent). In fifth place were coloured immigrants, up from 46 per cent to 57 per cent. When asked who were chiefly to blame for the riots, the largest proportion blamed both whites and coloured people but where one group was blamed, it tended to be coloured people. Despite the disturbances, comparisons with a study in 1964 suggested that coloured people had become more acceptable as friends, neighbours and workmates. One side effect of the disturbances was increased unease about the police, with one in three of the public saying that something had happened to make them feel uneasy. The public were also ill at ease about the rising crime rate, nine in ten believing that crime was increasing and one in two of these people blamed unemployment as the main reason. The April riots in Brixton were followed by further riots in Toxteth. When asked how important various causes could be in the increase in crime and violence, a general breakdown in respect for authority topped the list, mentioned as being very important by two in three of the public, followed by the level of unemployment, laws being too lenient and poor parental examples. The public were also critical about the efficiency of the church, with around one in three thinking it was not giving adequate answers to the problems of our society, nor to the problems of family life, nor to man's spiritual needs.

In mid-September Mrs Thatcher reshuffled her Cabinet, getting rid of some of its members and bringing in Cecil Parkinson as party chairman. Two in three of the public felt that the Conservatives had not kept their election promises and the top three broken promises among these people were unemployment, taxation and inflation. In by-elections, Mr Jenkins for the SDP almost won the safe Labour seat of Warrington, while Mrs Shirley Williams triumphed in the supposedly safe Conservative seat of Crosby. Gallup's October voting study put the Liberals and the SDP combined at 40 per cent, with both the Conservatives and Labour below

30 per cent in the share of votes. By December support for the Alliance was up to 50.5 per cent, the highest post war level for a third party. At the same time support for Labour had fallen to 23.5 per cent and for the Conservatives to 23 per cent, their lowest points since the war, and Mrs Thatcher became the least liked prime minister over the same period, with just 25 per cent satisfied with her.

As a contrast to the public's opinions about hard core political matters, people were also asked questions about paranormal behaviour and about the 'smallest room in the house'. One in ten, for example, claimed to have seen a ghost and one in four had paid to have their fortune told. Majorities believed in forecasting future events, deja vu and in thought-transference. Substantial minorities also believed in faith-healing, hypnotism, life after death, ghosts or flying saucers. A more down-to-earth study was conducted for Crown Paints - on the British toilet, though one in four of the public called it the 'loo'. Around one in five toilets had a chain pull flush and more than half of the toilets were less than two square yards. Again, just over half the public had a separate toilet, two in three had one as part of a combined bathroom, and a little over one in two were heated. One in two toilets had a mirror and one in five had some greenery. The most frequent activities, apart from the obvious, were thinking or reading. One in five members of the public liked the idea of having a heated seat in the fantasy toilet of their dreams, or a built-in stereo.

1982

It became obvious that the level of support for the Liberals and the SDP would not stay at its high point for very long - media impact being necessary to keep the new alliance in the public's view. Even in January 1982, for example, although the Alliance was still 10 points ahead of Labour and 12 points ahead of the Conservatives, their massive advantage of December had more than halved and was destined to disappear altogether by March. This recovery by the Conservatives was against a background of increasing unemployment - passing 3 million - and Roy Jenkins winning the Hillhead by-election for the SDP.

In early April Argentina invaded the Falklands and the British political scene was once more transformed: unemployment was still considered the most urgent problem facing the country - by 47 per cent - but 'international affairs' emerged as the second concern, mentioned by 27 per cent of the public. When asked which party could best handle the urgent problems, a 6-point lead in March for Labour was reversed and the Conservatives took a 3-point lead in April. By mid-May the Conservatives had taken a 12.5

points lead in party support over the Alliance, with Labour in third place 13.5 points adrift. Mrs Thatcher's personal standing went from 35 per cent in April to 44 per cent in May, while Mr Foot's standing declined from 23 per cent to 18 per cent over the same period. At the same time, international affairs were a close second behind unemployment - 42 per cent and 45 per cent respectively - as the most urgent problems facing the country. With the defeat of the Argentinians on the Falklands, the Conservatives stood at 46.5 per cent in July, 19 points ahead of Labour and 22.5 points ahead of the Alliance - in sharp contrast to the position in December 1981.

A very British topic was studied in April: social attitudes, with particular emphasis on the class system. The public, for example, emerged as a distrustful group, with more than one in two thinking that 'you can't be too careful in dealing with people'. When asked which of various groups of people they would not like to have as neighbours, heavy drinkers (49 per cent) were top of the list of undesirables, closely followed by people with a criminal record (42 per cent). The least disliked, of the 11 groups offered, were students (9 per cent) and unmarried mothers (5 per cent). People were also asked to rate what helped in making a successful marriage. Top of the thirteen items measured was 'understanding and tolerance', with 85 per cent rating it as 'very important', closely followed by 'faithfulness' (83 per cent) and 'mutual respect and understanding' (82 per cent). Least importance was attached to 'agreement on politics', with only 6 per cent thinking it was very important, and 80 per cent thinking it was not very important that the couple were from the same social background, the topic of the bulk of the remaining questions. Although just one in four thought that the public was 'very aware' of social differences in Britain, twice as many (51 per cent) thought that a person's social class affected their opportunities 'a lot'. On the other hand, one in two thought that there were less differences between the social classes than in the past, while around one in four thought that class differences had widened. Finally, people were asked questions about potential aids to close the gap. Six in ten, for example, said that their children mixed with children from other social classes, though one in three said they did not. The public were evenly divided on private education: 43 per cent being interested in it if they could afford it but 49 per cent were not interested in sending their children to a fee-paying school. There was also some reluctance to have their children acquire the speaking and accent of another class.

The year 1982 was also marked by that other typically British past-time, football, with the World Soccer Championship taking place in Spain. Neither the English nor the Scots gave their national teams much chance in the competition - 18 per cent and 15 per cent respectively thinking their teams would win. As it turned out, both public's nationalism was tempered by more than a touch of realism.

In July the public were asked to rate 19 social values on a scale of importance, where zero meant extremely unimportant and ten meant extremely important. Four items achieved a score of 9 or more out of 10: having a good family life, being in good physical health, personal satisfaction or happiness, and freedom of choice to do what they want. At the bottom, with a score of just under 5 (out of 10), was taking part in church-related activities.

In the same month Roy Jenkins defeated David Owen for the SDP leadership. The public's initial rating of the new leader was relatively good with 50 per cent thinking he would prove a good leader, 11 points down on Mr Steel's own rating but more than triple Mr Foot's. Within a few months the rating of Mr Jenkins had fallen to just one in three, with almost as many prophesying that he would not prove a good leader. The following month, when asked to rate the honesty and ethical standards of various professions, Members of Parliament overall were given a poor rating, with only 15 per cent thinking they had high ethical standards. This was equalled by journalists and was only slightly bettered by trade union leaders, building contractors and advertising executives. Top of the professions came doctors with a 75 per cent 'high' standards rating and police officers with 56 per cent.

In September Gallup asked a number of questions about test-tube babies and surrogate mothers. Ninety-five per cent of the public said that they were aware of the concept, a very high level of (claimed) awareness, and two in three of this group approved of the basic idea. The public were less supportive, however, of some of the details of the test-tube method. They disapproved on balance of the idea of freezing unused fertilised eggs for future use and disapproved by a bigger margin of surrogate mothers. When it came to the moral dilemma of who should keep the baby born to a surrogate mother, who then decided she wanted the baby herself, five in ten said that it should remain with the mother, while two in ten thought it should be given to the couple whose fertilised egg was used. On balance, more people approved of the idea of giving a fertilised egg from one couple to another married couple who could not have children so that they could, than disapproved.

The year ended with a rather mixed bag of surveys, the first dealing with group influence. When asked, for example, how much influence 'people like yourself' have on Britain's future, only 8 per cent thought that they had a lot of influence, 38 per cent said 'a little' and 50 per cent felt that they had no influence at all. This compared with 78 per cent thinking that the Prime Minister had a lot of influence, big business (68 per cent) and the trade unions (62 per cent). In 1976 the trade unions were thought to have had a lot of influence by 85 per cent of the public.

The second of the three studies asked people what they thought was the ideal size of a family, one of Gallup's longest-running questions. One per cent thought that there should be no children and 2 per cent thought that 1 child was sufficient, but 70 per cent felt that husband, wife and 2 children was the ideal. Overall this worked out as an average of 2.4 children compared with the 1939 average of 2.9 children. Then, 25 per cent mentioned four or more children as being the ideal. People were also asked, as 3 years earlier, what their family spent on food in the average week and what they thought was the ideal income for a family of four, including two children. Compared with 1979, the amount spent on food had risen from £25 per week to £30, while the ideal income had mushroomed from £90 a week to £141.

The final survey dealt with road accidents, another topic that Gallup have been tracking for a number of years. In 1982 44 per cent of the public said that they had been involved in a road accident at some time, compared with 37 per cent in 1976. In both studies around one in four drivers said that they had been stopped for speeding. This was in contrast to the higher speeds being achieved by drivers over the six year period: in 1976, for example, 33 per cent said that in the previous 12 months they had driven at speeds in excess of 70mph, including 6 per cent in the 'ton-up club'. By 1982 the proportion driving in excess of 70mph had risen to 47 per cent, with 9 per cent in excess of 100mph. They had, however, become more safety conscious. In 1976 one in four (27 per cent) drivers said that they wore a safety belt all the time while driving, but this proportion had risen to 44 per cent six years later.

1983

The new year began with unemployment still dominating the list of urgent problems, though with the Conservatives comfortably ahead of Labour in voting support and with the Alliance in a relatively poor third place. The public were evenly divided on whether there should be an election in the near future or not, but when it came to who would win the next election, then an unknown date, six in ten said that the Conservatives would remain in power. Given the gift of hindsight and the impact of the defence issue in the 1983 election, it is perhaps worthwhile to look at various questions Gallup asked in the early part of 1983 on nuclear weapons and related topics. Although one in two of the British public thought that Russia was most likely to start a nuclear attack in Europe, 28 per cent thought that the US would strike first, and one in two thought it at least 'somewhat likely' that the hostile attitudes between America and Russia would escalate into a third world war. When asked whether they favoured or opposed a move towards neutralism in Western Europe, 45 per cent were in favour and slightly fewer, 42 per cent, opposed.

In a separate study, 46 per cent felt that there would be a third world war at some time in the future and four in ten of these felt that it would happen within the next decade. A majority (58 per cent) of the general public felt that it would be a nuclear war, though a perhaps hopeful 28 per cent thought that only conventional weapons would be employed. One in four (28 per cent) were also 'very worried' that a world war would break out in which nuclear bombs would be used. This compared with the 12 per cent in 1964 who thought there would be a world war using atomic and/or hydrogen bombs. Similarly, 28 per cent supported the idea of unilateralism but 65 per cent were opposed. On the other hand, only 32 per cent thought the new American-controlled cruise nuclear missiles should be based in Britain and 54 per cent were opposed. The Conservatives, however, by a margin of 41 per cent to 16 per cent, were thought to be the party best able to handle the problem of nuclear weapons.

Another 'plus' policy for the Conservatives was taxation. At the end of February people were asked whether taxation would be increased or cut in the Budget. While 26 per cent thought that taxation would be increased, slightly more (33 per cent) thought that it would be cut. In 1982 the figures had been 46 per cent and 15 per cent respectively. The public, however, took a cynical view about the possibility of tax cuts: one in two thought that the Budget would be especially generous for election purposes, in sharp contrast to the less than one in five who felt that way about the 1965, non-election Budget. Naturally, three in four of the public approved of the increases in personal tax allowances in the 1983 Budget and a little over one in two thought that it was, overall, a fair one.

People in March were asked to look forward to the turn of the century and to say whether certain events would have happened. A similar question had also been asked in 1959 about the future. Most Britons (61 per cent) in the 1983 study expected a three-day week by the year 2000, compared with 13 per cent in the earlier survey. There was also a majority (66 per cent) expecting that a cure for cancer would have been found, virtually the same (65 per cent) as 24 years before; and the view that life expectancy would have increased to 100 years was held by 33 per cent, the same as in 1959.

And so the election came around. A disastrous local argument in Bermondsey 'gave' the seat to the Liberals in a by-election, but Labour managed to hold Darlington in a later by-election, with the SDP candidate coming a poor third. The local elections on 5 May confirmed the Conservatives' advantage and 9 June was selected for the general election. As far as the opinion polls were concerned, there were only two questions in the 1983 campaign: by how much would the Conservatives win and who would be in second place? A little under one in three in April thought that the publication of opinion polls should be banned during an election, but slightly more than one in two took the opposite view. A survey conducted on election day itself and the preceding Wednesday found 5 per cent of electors saying that they had been influenced by the polls. The top issues considered to be most important by voters in the election were unemployment (72 per cent), defence (38 per cent) and prices (20 per cent). Mention has already been made about the particularly poor ratings of Michael Foot and the declining popularity of Roy Jenkins, accentuated during the election campaign, and it was perhaps inevitable that both leaders were to be replaced before the year was out.

As a contrast to the intense political polling conducted during the early months of 1983, questions were repeated from 1967 on what was worrying people. 'Keeping your (your husband's) job' caused 'a lot' of worry to 24 per cent of the public, compared with just 7 per cent 16 years earlier. The degree to which other things worried the public a lot were 'making both ends meet' (21 per cent in 1983 and 20 per cent in 1967), 'possibility of another war' (20 per cent and 10 per cent respectively), 'having a reasonable place to live in' (20 per cent and 10 per cent), 'your health' (20 per cent and 14 per cent), 'having enough money in your old age' (14 per cent in each year) and 'getting proper food' (13 per cent and 8 per cent). Thus, concern about a number of these items had increased significantly since the late 1960s. The first post-election Gallup survey put the parties basically where they had been a month earlier, but Dr David Owen had replaced Roy Jenkins as leader of the SDP and 55 per cent thought that he would do a good job. The most urgent problem facing the country, as far as the public were concerned, remained unemployment. In August a number of questions, first asked in 1968, about European countries were repeated and showed some quite distinct changes in attitudes. On a question, for example, of who were Britain's friends in Europe, West Germany emerged top in 1983 with 40 per cent mentions, followed by Holland (23 per cent) and France (20 per cent). In the 1968 study, Holland (35 per cent) and Denmark (32 per cent) topped the list, with West Germany (23 per cent) in sixth place and France (11 per cent) in eighth. The passing of 15 years also showed the effect of tourism in terms of which countries people had ever visited. In 1968 France had been the country most Britons had visited, mentioned by 32 per cent. By 1983 the proportion had increased to 53 per cent. Perhaps the biggest change had been in visits to Spain, rising from only 12 per cent in 1968 to 38 per cent in 1983. Despite all this foreign travel, however, we stubbornly refused to talk in anything but the mother tongue. In 1968 18 per cent said that they could speak another language sufficiently well enough to make sense of a newspaper written in that language. After 15 years the proportion remained virtually unchanged at 19 per cent.

The voting patterns were shaken up somewhat in October when Neil Kinnock took over as Labour leader from Michael Foot. He, too, like David Owen before him, scored high in the public's initial rating, with 58 per cent thinking that he would prove a good leader. Support for the party at the same time gained 11 points, though they still lagged behind the victorious Conservatives. The boost to Labour due to the change in leadership could also be seen in the replies to other questions. The proportion, for example, who agreed with the statement 'Labour leadership is poor now' dropped from 87 per cent to 37 per cent within 2 months, and whereas 75 per cent who had seen Michael Foot on television thought he had not increased support for the Labour party, 71 per cent who had seen Neil Kinnock on television thought that he had.

One of the policies Mrs Thatcher and the Conservative party had campaigned for was the privatisation of public organisations, such as British Telecom, British Gas, etc. In late October people were asked their attitudes towards the proposed privatisation of British Telecom. On balance the public were against the idea, 39 per cent thinking it was a good idea and 46 per cent a bad idea. Those thinking it was a good idea put forward four main reasons: it would bring more competition, they felt that it would lead to a better service, they believed in private enterprise and they thought that prices would either stabilise or actually go down. The top four reasons given by the opponents of privatisation were that B T was a profit-making concern, that the service would deteriorate, that the profits should go to the public and that prices would rise.

Britain's membership of the Common Market had not only changed the public's view of Europe but had also forced them to reappraise their view of the Commonwealth. In 1961, for example, 48 per cent thought that the Commonwealth was more important to Britain than either America (19 per cent) or Europe (18 per cent). Twenty-two years later Europe came top with 39 per cent, with America (26 per cent) and the Commonwealth (25 per cent) vying for second place. Even greater changes had taken place in attitudes towards permanent homes for members of the Royal Family in Commonwealth countries. In 1954 60 per cent thought that this would be a good thing, but only 28 per cent did so in 1983. America, too, had been in the news following their invasion of Grenada. Although the action had been warmly received both in Grenada and in America, a majority (55 per cent) of the British public disapproved.

1984

It would have been unthinkable to let 1984 pass without some reference to Orwell's famous book of the same name. One in four of the public claimed to have read the book and one in five had seen either a film or a television version based on it. A little over two in five felt that Britain since 1948 had moved in the direction of Orwell's imaginary world: under totalitarian rule with personal freedom eliminated and the citizens under the tyranny of 'Big Brother'. In the same study majorities agreed with the statements 'there is no real privacy because the government can learn anything it wants about you' (59 per cent), 'people are asked to make sacrifices but government officials themselves live in luxury' (59 per cent) and 'the government uses false words and statistics to hide bad news about the economy and the quality of life' (57 per cent). On the other hand, three in four of the public felt that the British had 'a great deal of freedom' Having perhaps more Marxist overtones than Orwellian, was the finding in March of the growing proportion of the public who felt that there was a 'class struggle' in Britain. In 1961, when the question had first been asked, 56 per cent thought that there was, but by 1984 the proportion had risen to 74 per cent.

The health of the public was a topic also returned to when questions were repeated from 1956. Cancer was still the top disease or complaint that people thought about, though its relative position as a killer disease had changed: in 1956, 14 per cent said that they thought about cancer, rising to 20 per cent in 1984. In both studies two in three of the public said that there was no particular disease or complaint that they thought about. When asked, however, which complaint killed most people in Britain, heart troubles (53 per cent) topped the list, followed by cancer (39 per cent). In 1956 the position had been reversed, with 14 per cent and 41 per cent respectively. Although attitudes may have changed in the 18 years between the two studies, behaviour had not. Visits to a doctor, for example, showed hardly any change: one in two of the public in both studies said that they had visited a doctor in the previous 6 months. Similarly, a little under one in three on both occasions said that they had bought some medicines from a chemist rather than bothering to go to a doctor.

Comparisons even further back, in fact with 1942, reinforced the picture of the changing relationship between Britain and the United States. In 1984 61 per cent agreed with the statement 'they [the Americans] take a superior attitude towards the British and they have no grounds for this', compared with 37 per cent in 1942. More people also agreed (43 per cent) in 1984 than in 1942 (28 per cent) that 'the Americans are too willing to let other people fight for them'. On the other hand, fewer agreed with the statements 'they are a more democratic people than we are' (36 per cent and 52 per cent respectively) and 'we would be better off if we were more like the Americans in many respects' (24 per cent and 41 per cent respectively). Even the public's perception of American goods had significantly changed over time. When asked in 1960 which of a number of countries produced goods of high quality, America came top, selected by 62 per cent of the British people. In 1984, the figure had dropped to only 22 per cent, putting America in fifth place overall. When asked which of the nine most recent presidents would be remembered as the best, John F. Kennedy topped the list, while Richard Nixon came top as the one who would be remembered as the worst president.

Majorities of the British in 1984 were satisfied with 'the amount of leisure and free time you get to yourself' (80 per cent), 'your housing situation' (79 per cent), 'the standard of living of yourself and family' (70 per cent), 'the work you do' (66 per cent) and 'your family income' (54 per cent). But majorities were dissatisfied with 'the honesty and standards of behaviour of people in this country today' (73 per cent) and 'the position of Britain in the world today' (56 per cent). In a separate study, 34 per cent said that they were 'very satisfied' with their life as a whole and 54 per cent were 'fairly satisfied'.

Despite the publicity in 1984 leading up to the election for Members of the European Parliament and the lack of a competing general election, a feature in 1979, awareness of the 'Europoll' was no better than it had been 5 years earlier and few people said that they would vote. In a study conducted in early June 70 per cent said that they had heard something recently about the European Parliament and 41 per cent said that it was to do with the election. In 1979 the figures had been 77 per cent and 42 per cent respectively. When asked how likely they were to vote in the election, 39 per cent said they would, compared with 43 per cent in 1979. The public were also slightly less interested in the outcome of the election - the party strength in the new European Parliament.

The year saw the start of one of the longest-running miners' strikes and, in contrast to the 1974 dispute, the public did not take the miners' side. In 1974, by a margin of two to one, the public had supported the miners, but in 1984 the public were on balance inclined to support the employers. Public disapproval of the miners' methods in the dispute, leading to violent clashes with the police, was also higher in 1984 than it had been 10 years earlier. As the dispute wore on through the year, the proportion mentioning strikes as the most urgent problem facing the country increased, from 9 per cent in April to 32 per cent in September. Unemployment, however, still dominated the public's list of perceived problems and a question asked in July highlighted their concern. In 1965 46 per cent thought that children of people like themselves would find a job without any trouble, 42 per cent thought that there would be some difficulty but that they would find a job in the end, and 4 per cent thought that finding a job would prove almost impossible. Almost 20 years later the pattern of replies had been reversed. In 1984 only 4 per cent said that there would be no problem in finding a job, 54 per cent saw some difficulty and 39 per cent thought that it would be well-nigh impossible.

There can be little doubt that the growth in unemployment and the government's apparent lack of success (some would say lack of effort) in stemming the rise contributed to a deep feeling of alienation and to the concept of the 'two nations'. In July eight in ten of the public said that they felt that 'the rich get richer and the poor get poorer'. Fewer, but still majorities, felt that 'most people with power try to take advantage of people like yourself' (62 per cent), 'the people running the country don't really care what happens to you' (58 per cent) and 'what you think doesn't count very much any more' (56 per cent). A little over one in three thought that they were left out of things going on around them. While three in ten thought that the government's views were representative of the views of the general public as a whole, twice as many thought that they were not.

Three months later, in October, around six in ten of the public said that they thought of British society as being divided into two halves, the haves and the have-nots. Although a majority (53 per cent) felt that everyone who tries had a chance to succeed, 40 per cent thought that British society deliberately excluded some kinds of people from a chance to make a good living. The public took a negative view of the government on this issue, 62 per cent thinking that their policies were aimed at helping the haves and only 7 per cent aimed at helping the have-nots. At the same time, people were asked to rate their neighbourhood - on a scale from 0 to 10 - at that point in time, five years before and five years in the future. With a score of 10 representing their ideal neighbourhood, people gave their neighbourhood a score of 7.4 for five years before, dropping to 7.0 for the present and an even lower 6.3 for five years in the future.

This pessimism about their neighbourhood in the future was reflected in the public's pessimism about Britain's future generally. Two in three (65 per cent), for example, thought it likely that 'riots and civil disturbances in our cities will be common events', 57 per cent that 'acts of political terrorism in Britain will become common events' and 50 per cent that 'the police in our cities will find it impossible to protect our personal safety on the streets'. As an indication of the public's disenchantment with nuclear energy, 41 per cent thought it likely that 'there will be a serious accident at a British nuclear power station'.

Questions on a possibly more down-to-earth topic were asked in late October - a relaxation in the licensing laws. On balance, the public took the view that the opening hours of public houses were not long enough, although two in three felt that the hours were about right. Around six in ten of the public approved of the idea of the total number of opening hours remaining the same but the publican being allowed to open and close as he wished. The same proportion, however, did not want to see public houses open in the afternoon, possibly seeing it as an unwarranted extension of opening hours. A majority (55 per cent) also approved if opening hours on Sundays were made the same as for weekdays, and even more, eight in ten, approved of the idea of allowing restaurants to supply drinks with meals at all times of day and night. On the effect of a relaxation in the licensing laws, 35 per cent thought that it would lead to more drunkenness and problems of drink, but 44 per cent felt that it would not and 17 per cent felt that it would actually reduce the problems.

The ordination of women in the Church continued to be a controversial topic for the bishops, and in fact was coming to the fore again in 1987 as this book was being written. Despite the heated arguments in the Church itself, two in three of the general public thought that the Church of England should accept women as priests and bishops. Asked about the gospel miracles, 25 per cent felt that they were mostly historical facts, 38 per cent thought that they were mostly the gospel writers' interpretations of certain events and 26 per cent saw them as mostly legends. On the question of whether Christ was born of a virgin, 35 per cent thought that this was a historical fact, but 46 per cent thought it to be a legend. On another controversial subject, two in three of the public said that the Church should not take sides in political issues.

The miners' strike was still in operation at the end of the year, though the public were less likely to mention strikes as an urgent problem facing the country. As far as the public was concerned, none of the personalities involved in the dispute emerged with any significant degree of distinction, particularly Mr Scargill and to a lesser degree, Mr MacGregor. On a more basic topic, the pound note was replaced by a pound coin, though three in four of the public preferred the traditional note.

Gallup also repeated some questions from the late 1940s to see how things in Britain had changed. In 1984, for example, 84 per cent thought that their neighbours were 'mainly pleasant' compared with 68 per cent who took the same view in 1948. We were also more likely than in 1948 to take in messages or parcels for our neighbours, have them in our homes, lend them things, do shopping for them, or look after their children - a contrast to the nostalgic view of the close-knit community in earlier times. In a question of separate schooling or co-education for children aged over eleven, the overwhelming majority, eight in ten, in 1984 thought that they should be educated together. In 1948 the public was almost evenly divided on the topic. The modern-day public is more proficient in basic skills than their counterparts of the 1940s. Two in three said that they could swim compared with one in two making that claim in 1949. There are also more chess players (29 per cent and 18 per cent respectively) and, naturally, given the increase in car ownership, more people who can drive (63 per cent and 37 per cent respectively). Men still preferred to be men, around 9 in 10 so choosing if given the choice, and women were more likely than in 1947 to want to be a woman. In 1947 56 per cent of women said they would rather be a woman, rising to 75 per cent in 1984. Again compared also with 1947, we were just as likely to take sleeping pills, around one in six in both studies, though in 1984 we were less likely to find it difficult to get up in the morning - 30 per cent saying they had difficulty against 42 per cent in 1947.

1985

The year 1984 having passed with none of the dire consequences predicted by George Orwell 36 years previously, 1985 opened on a none-too-happy situation. The miners' strike was still in full flood, with the National Coal Board warning that 50,000 mining jobs could be lost to deteriorating pits. At the same time, the pound fell to a new low against the dollar of $1.1185 and, for the first time since 1981, the Bank of England imposed a minimum lending rate. Unemployment remained firmly in the public's mind as the most urgent problem facing the country, though the Conservatives were clear favourites to win the next election.

One of the first major topics to be covered in the new year was education, with the public seeing falling standards of discipline at school, falling standards of achievement and falling educational standards generally. When asked what the relative emphasis should be for various subjects, the three Rs - reading, writing and arithmetic - dominated the public's syllabus, followed by science and foreign languages. On the other hand, sizeable minorities thought that three subjects in particular should not be taught at all: anti-sexism studies (25 per cent), anti-racism studies (18 per cent) and peace studies (14 per cent). On a lighter note, one in four of the public said that they had made a New Year resolution, the top two being to give up or to cut down on smoking and to go on a diet.

In February Gallup asked for the first time a number of questions about President Reagan's Strategic Defence Initiative, popularly known as 'Star Wars'. Nine in ten of the British public were aware of the system by then but just 41 per cent knew enough about it to correctly identify it as a means of defence against a nuclear missile attack. A similar proportion, only 39 per cent, thought that such a system would actually work, with slightly more (43 per cent) thinking that it would not. The public were also evenly divided on whether or not to agree to a ban on space weapons in talks with the Russians. A little over one in three thought that the West should agree to such a ban, to avoid a dangerous arms race, but the same proportion felt that the West would forfeit a technological advantage to do so. Three in four of the public, however, took the view that 'space should be kept free of all weapons'.

In March, against a background of a weakening pound, four in ten of the public described Britain's economic health as good, but six in ten thought that it was poor, with almost nine in ten thinking that the American dollar was a strong currency. Three in four of this latter group felt that a strong dollar was a bad thing for Britain. At the same time, questions were asked on an associated topic - poverty in Britain. Three in four of the public felt that the proportion of British people living below the poverty line was increasing year to year, and the same proportion thought that the money and wealth in Britain should be more evenly distributed among a larger group of the people. It is perhaps of little surprise, therefore, that the public were taking a more sympathetic view towards the poor in 1985. Eight years earlier, 33 per cent thought that lack of effort was often to blame if a person was poor, 30 per cent put it down to circumstances beyond the person's control and 31 per cent felt that it was a combination of the two. By 1985 the figures were 21 per cent, 49 per cent and 28 per cent respectively.

Mention has been made elsewhere in this chapter of the changing perception of health risks, from cancer to heart problems, but in March, for the first time, Gallup began to monitor the public's awareness and perception of the killer disease AIDS (Acquired Immune Deficiency Syndrome). Virtually the whole adult population were aware of AIDS by March and six in ten of these saw its spread as a matter of great concern and two in three knew that homosexuals were the group most at risk. Naturally, nine in ten of those aware of AIDS approved of the idea of male blood donors being asked if they were a practising homosexual.

A number of questions were asked in May about government spending, the Welfare State and the National Health Service. Firstly, people were asked which items of government spending they would give highest priority to for extra spending. The top three items were health (38 per cent), education (18 per cent) and help for industry (17 per cent). When it came to government spending on social benefits, top priority was given to retirement pensions (40 per cent), followed by benefits for the disabled (24 per cent). Amid talk of scroungers on the State, people were asked whether they agreed or disagreed with two statements about benefits. Around two thirds (68 per cent) agreed that 'large numbers of people these days falsely claim benefits', but even more, 85 per cent, agreed that 'large numbers of people who are eligible for benefits these days fail to claim them'. The public, however, were more evenly divided on the question of the level of benefits for the unemployed: 41 per cent thought that they were too low and caused hardship, while 32 per cent felt that they were too high and discouraged people from finding jobs. Awareness of the government's plans to review the Welfare State was reasonably high, 62 per cent having heard or read about them. Among those aware, the plans received a relatively poor reception - 59 per cent thought that they were a bad thing and 45 per cent saw themselves as being worse off in the long run. On a suggestion that the National Health Service should be available only to those people with low incomes, 60 per cent opposed the idea, though 34 per cent supported it.

In October 1982 a European-wide survey on attitudes towards the environment had taken place and the questions were repeated in Britain in May 1985. People in both studies were asked how worried they were about a number of environmental problems, and concern on all of the nine issues measured had increased over the three year period. Top of the list came the disposal of nuclear waste (66 per cent expressing 'a great deal' of concern), the disposal of industrial chemical waste (57 per cent) and damage caused to sea life and beaches by spillage or discharge by oil tankers (55 per cent). In 1982, the figures had been 52 per cent, 45 per cent and 45 per cent respectively. The public were also more likely to consider protecting the environment as more important than either keeping prices down or economic growth. The environmentalists, for example, increased from around one in two to three in five.

A study in mid-July dealt with the fears and aspirations of a sample of young people aged 15 or 16 who were still at school, rather than the public as a whole. One in fourteen of this group said that they never read a daily newspaper and more than twice as many never read a Sunday newspaper. When it came to the broadcast media, one in twenty never watched a news broadcast on television and three in ten never listened to the news on the radio. They were reasonably satisfied with the education they had received - 59 per cent being either 'completely satisfied' or 'satisfied' - but 71 per cent felt that it would be, at best, 'fairly difficult' to find their first job, with 20 per cent expecting it to take at least a year. More than nine in ten agreed that 'everybody should have the right to a job' and 32 per cent agreed with the rather chilling concept that 'the use of violence is sometimes justified in bringing about political change'.

In August questions were repeated from July 1963 about the idea of a fixed link across the English Channel. As well as becoming cool to our membership of the Common Market, opposition to the link among the British had increased. In 1963 69 per cent thought that Britain should support the idea and 17 per cent thought otherwise. By 1985 the figures had changed to 50 per cent and 37 per cent respectively. Despite this decline in support for the general idea, given a choice between a tunnel or a bridge, a tunnel emerged as the public's choice, as it had in 1963. One in four of the public (over ten million adults) in 1985 said that they had crossed the Channel to France with a car by ferry or hovercraft in the previous 5 years.

In September and October 1985 a number of questions were asked about violence, with nine in ten of the public thinking that crimes of violence were a very serious social problem in Britain. A general breakdown in respect for authority and the use of drugs were thought to be very important causes for the increase in crime and violence by two in three of the public. The public were almost evenly divided on how violent a country Britain was - 48 per cent thinking that it was at least 'a fairly violent country' and 51 per cent who thought that it was 'not a particularly violent country' or 'not a violent country at all'. Nevertheless, nine in ten thought that there was more violence than five years earlier. Television came in for criticism in its depiction of violence: 61 per cent said that TV violence was harmful to society, and 45 per cent that TV news gave too much attention to violent crimes and that TV news reporting exaggerated the amount of violence in the country. Three in five felt that there was too much violence in TV entertainment shows, though slightly more thought that violent scenes were sometimes necessary to tell a good story.

More questions on AIDS were added to the repertoire in September and again in November, following the death from the disease of film actor, Rock Hudson. Around one in three of the public were worried that they or someone they knew would get AIDS, and one in two felt that it was at least somewhat likely that it would eventually become an epidemic for the public at large. Around two in three, however, admitted that they either knew little or nothing at all about the disease. This was reflected in the replies to a question on how AIDS could be caught. Three in ten thought that you could catch AIDS through kissing someone, 23 per cent by using the same drinking glass, 17 per cent by being sneezed on, 17 per cent by sitting on a toilet seat and 5 per cent by shaking hands!

1986

There can be little doubt that the beginning of 1986 was dominated by the events surrounding the Westland helicopter company, leading first to the resignation of Michael Heseltine, Secretary of State for Defence, to be followed soon after by Leon Brittan, Secretary of State for Trade and Industry. In contrast to a year earlier, Gallup's first published poll showed the Conservatives in third place, 9.5 points down on their January 1985 level of support. Labour were still in second place, just one point up on a year earlier, while the Alliance were ahead with 35 per cent, 9.5 points up on their support a year before. At the same time, Mrs Thatcher's personal popularity fell to 31 per cent, just one point above her worst figure since the 1983 general election. On the other hand, the standings of David Steel and David Owen were on the upswing in January, but Neil Kinnock's was declining, despite the government's obvious discomforts. Another January study emerged with the public believing that Mr Churchill would be remembered as the best of our recent prime ministers and that Mrs Thatcher would be remembered as the worst.

Later that month the public were asked to rate the importance of 20 potential policies, ranging across the Health Service to unilateralism, redistribution of wealth to environmental protection, and from captital punishment to overseas aid. Only for two of the policies did a majority think that it was very important that it should be done: three in four thought that putting more money into the Health Service was that important and a little over one in two wanted increased public spending to reduce unemployment. One in two also felt that it was very important that council tenants should have the right to buy their homes and that capital punishment should be reintroduced. Slightly fewer, around four in ten, rated spending more money on tackling pollution of the air and rivers as very important, as were measures to promote equal opportunities for women and firm guidelines for wage and price rises. On the other hand, four in ten thought it very important that we should not give up Britain's nuclear weapons, whatever other countries decided. Very similar results also emerged when the questions were repeated in mid-November.

On 24 and 25 March US fighter aircraft attacked Libyan coastal missile launch sites after US aircraft had been fired upon in international waters in the Gulf of Sirte. Three weeks later, on 15 April, US bombers, some based in Britain, attacked targets in Tripoli and Benghazi. While a little over one in four Britons approved of the March action, one in two disapproved. At the same time, approval of America's role in world affairs dropped from a little over one in three approving to around one in four, but climbed back to one in three after the April raids. By a margin of a little over two to one, the British public disapproved of this later action. Two in three thought that the government had been wrong to allow the Americans to use air bases in Britain for their attacks, four in five felt that it would lead to more terrorist attacks in Britain and one in two thought that Britain's long-term interests had been badly served.

Of perhaps greater long-term concern was the explosion at a nuclear power plant in Chernobyl, near Kiev, Russia. It had become evident in surveys that the British public had become hostile to nuclear energy in the decade before the Chernobyl incident and the accident accelerated this downward trend. In May 1976, for example, one in three said that they would oppose the building of a nuclear power station in their area and this gradually rose to a little under one in two, but then jumped to almost two in three after the accident in Russia. Later studies during the year, however, showed a decline in hostility, easing back to the earlier, pre-accident levels.

A facet of the 1980s was the appeal of the concept of 'healthy living' - exercising , 'natural' foods, etc. In a study in late May, a little over four in ten of the public said that they were taking less or no sugar with their meals, were eating less or no fried or fatty foods, and eating more fruit and 'fibre' foods. A little over one in three were also cutting down on their intake of salt and butter, and one in four said that they were eating less or no red meat. In mid-June, another facet of British life was investigated - the growth of the 'plastic economy'. A little over one in two of the public said that they had a personal bank card, which allowed them to obtain cash, deposit cheques, pay bills, etc. Among those people with such a bank card, it accounted for roughly half their recent banking transactions.

Two other apparently non-related topics in June, though each containing a degree of superstition, were paranormal experiences and gambling. On the former, more than three in ten of the public said that they had had a premonition and two in ten of these people described it as a religious experience. A little over one in four also felt that the patterning of events in their life convinced them that in some strange way they were meant to happen and one in three of these described this as a religious experience. Around one in four of the public said that they had been aware at sometime of the presence of God or that they were receiving help in answer to prayer, and, naturally, eight in ten of these saw this as a religious experience. In the study of gambling, one in three said that they did the football pools, and around one in ten used a bookmaker, paid to play bingo, or played dice or cards for money. Around two in three of the gamblers reckoned that they had lost money in the previous 12 months, one in six felt that they had probably just about broke even, and only one in ten thought that they were ahead of the game.

A few questions were asked in July on a non-terrestial matter - space travel. The first of these dealt with which of the two super-powers were ahead in space developments. In 1972, the United States was mentioned by one in two people compared with two in ten for Russia. By 1986, however, Russia was thought to be ahead by almost one in two, while only one in three said it was the United States. The overwhelming majority of people, three in four, felt that the time and money spent on space programmes would do better being spent on problems nearer home, echoing the replies to the same question 15 years earlier. When asked whether, given the chance, they would like to travel into outer space, one in three said they would. The reversal of the replies in the first question was reflected to some degree in how the British public rated the two super-powers overall. In May 1978, using a scale ranging from +5 to -5, the United States scored +1.9, while Russia scored -1.9. By mid-1986 the figures were +1.0 and -0.4 respectively. Of the 12 countries rated in the 1986 study, Libya with -3.3 and South Africa with -2.4 were the most disliked.

In mid-year the Peacock Report made some recommendations about the future of broadcasting which were received with mixed feelings by the general public. More than eight in ten, for example, approved of the idea that pensioners drawing supplementary benefits should be exempt from the licence fee, while one in two approved of the recommendation that there should be no advertising on the BBC, and that the licence fee should be inflation-linked. Two in three, however, disapproved of a separate licence fee for car radios and around one in two disapproved of inflation-linked licence fees, the idea that BBC Radios 1 and 2 should be sold off and financed by advertising, and that television should be paid for by a 'pay-as-you-view' scheme in place of the annual licence fee.

Two nuclear issues were returned to in July: nuclear energy and nuclear weapons. On the former, people were asked whether they agreed or disagreed with 12 statements about the nuclear industry. Three in four of the public agreed with the statements 'nuclear plants are dangerous in that they produce radioactive waste' and 'the British nuclear power industry is too secretive'. Two in three also felt that there was not enough experience with nuclear plants and that they contaminated the surrounding areas with radioactivity. On the other hand, three in five disagreed that cooling towers had a negative effect on the local climate, and one in two disagreed that nuclear-based power is more economical and that nuclear plants are less damaging to the environment than other plants. To keep in touch with trends in attitudes towards nuclear weapons, Gallup repeated some questions from the summer of 1980. These showed significant changes of opinion over the intervening 6 years. The proportion, for example, who were worried about nuclear weapons and willing to do something about them had risen from 11 per cent to 17 per cent. Over the same period, the number of people who had been on an anti-nuclear demonstration had increased from 3 per cent to 6 per cent, and the number who had written a letter against nuclear weapons had gone from 1 per cent to 5 per cent. The proportion of people supporting the idea of unilateralism, though still a minority, had risen from 21 per cent in 1980 to 33 per cent. People in 1986 were less pessimistic about the chances of a nuclear war, however, than they had been in 1980, but were more pessimistic about their own chances of survival if Britain were to be attacked with nuclear weapons. This latter response was echoed in the replies to a question on Civil Defence. In 1980 61 per cent felt that Civil Defence made either little or no difference at all to people's chances of survival. It had risen to 73 per cent by 1986.

In September, as part of the celebrations to mark the fortieth anniversary of the British Market Research Society, Gallup repeated some questions from 1946. There were both some interesting differences and some interesting similarities in the results. In 1946, for example, 61 per cent of people said that there was a sewing machine in their home. Forty years on, the figure was hardly changed at 58 per cent. Fewer Britons in 1986 than in 1946 said that there were any superstitions they believed in - 26 per cent and 35 per cent respectively - yet more said that they sometimes 'touched wood'! We were more likely to be able to swim in 1986 than in 1946, more likely to be reading a book, but still taking pills with the same frequency. In 1946 the two most admired personalities had been Churchill and Montgomery. In 1986 it was the Queen and Mrs Thatcher. In fact, in 1946 the top four named had been men, whereas three of the top four in 1986 were women.

The following month a major study was conducted on 'The British Day', asking people questions about their activities during the average day from the moment they got up in the morning to putting their head back on the pillow at day's end. The best moment of the day was thought to be in the evening, particularly when coming home from work, and the worst moment was having to get up in the first place. The weekend days - Saturday, Sunday and Friday - were thought to be the best days of the week, while four in ten gave Monday as the worst. Sunday was the only other day to get into double figures (12 per cent) as a bad day. As a nation, the British appear to be very musical: four in ten claiming to sing to themselves every day or almost every day.

During the week one in two people relied on themselves to wake up, while four in ten used an alarm and one in ten were called. On Sundays, the self-reliant proportion increased to more than eight in ten. What time did people wake up? On a weekday, one in five were awake by 6 o'clock and a little over one in two by 7 o'clock. On a Sunday around one in three were awake by 7 o'clock and one in ten said that they did not get up until after 10 o'clock. Four in ten were sometimes given an early morning cup of tea or coffee in bed, with 16 per cent getting a daily cuppa. More than nine in ten women said that they made their own bed when they got up, compared with one in two men, four in ten of whom left it to their wives. One in three, when getting dressed, said that they took the weather forecasts into account, rising to two in five women. Two in three people had a breakfast during the week and three in four did so on a Sunday. Sixty per cent having a weekday breakfast had cereals and slightly fewer had toast (56 per cent). One in five started the day with an egg, and despite the growing availability of the 'continental breakfast', tea was the preferred breakfast beverage, mentioned by two in three taking breakfast. Coffee was drunk by one in four and was particularly popular with younger adults. A similar pattern emerged for the Sunday breakfasts, except that cooked breakfasts became more popular and fewer people had cereals. When it came to a weekday lunch, a little under one in two ate sandwiches, compared with one in three eating meat and one in five having a fish dish. Two in three said that they had a traditional roast for Sunday lunch most weekends, though one in eight never did so, including to one in five senior citizens.

In the evening 44 per cent said that they watched television before their main evening meal, rising to 76 per cent afterwards. Other evening activities, mentioned by around one in four people, were reading a newspaper, doing a job in the garden or around the home, reading a book, going for a drink at a pub, or visiting friends. We are not particularly sociable in Britain, with only one in four having friends over for a formal meal at least once a month. Four in ten never do so. Almost as many also never invite friends in for a drink and a little over one in four never offer an informal meal. Harking back to the musical note, one in five said that they sung in their bath or shower, while slightly fewer cut their toenails!

When asked what they most liked doing in bed, one in two said 'sleeping', the activity preferred most by all the groups in the survey. Among men, the runner-up was making love, followed by reading. For women, reading a book was more popular than love-making. One in three of all adults said that they wore nothing in bed during the summer and around one in four continued this practice in winter. When it came to sleep itself, one in three said that they woke up during the night most nights and 13 per cent said that on most nights they had a bad night's sleep. A little over one in four said that they dreamt most nights, though a mere 1 per cent suffered nightmares that often. One in ten took sleeping pills or tranquillizers before going to bed and this was significantly higher among the elderly.

Finally, what was a day at the office or factory like? One in four employed people said that they took work home to do in the evening, and this amounted to four in ten white collar workers. The figures were only slightly lower when people were asked about taking work home to do at the weekend. A car was the main means of getting to work - one in two employees using this method - and two in three workers claimed that they never arrived late for work. Four in ten of the men said that they had to wear a tie where they worked and a suit was obligatory for one in three men. A little under one in two workers felt that they were adequately paid for the work they did, but slightly more felt that they were not paid enough. The young, in particular, were disgruntled with their wages. While one in ten white collar workers thought that the work they did was boring, more than twice as many blue collar workers expressed boredom.

More questions were asked about AIDS in November, the replies to which showed increasing concern among the public about the disease. In March, for example, 66 per cent felt that the spread of the disease was a matter of great concern but it had risen to 85 per cent by November. Similarly, the proportion saying that it was very likely that AIDS would eventually become an epidemic for the public at large had increased from 24 per cent to 46 per cent over the same period. On the other hand, the public's knowledge of the disease was improving and fewer people thought that it could be contracted from kissing, using the same drinking glass or from sitting on a toilet seat.

To mark the festive season, questions were asked in mid-December about Christmas, some of which went back 30 years. Having a Christmas tree, for example, was much more likely in 1986 than it had been in 1953 - 79 per cent and 47 per cent respectively - though fewer people (52 per cent) said that they were having a family party (62 per cent in 1953). We were also buying more Christmas cards: the average number of cards bought in 1955 had been 24, rising to 32 in 1986. When asked how they regarded Christmas, around one in three of the public said it was mainly as a religious festival or an opportunity to meet family and friends. One in four saw it mainly as a holiday, while one in eight said it was mainly an occasion for eating and drinking. Three in four felt that Christmas was becoming less religious than it had been during their childhood.

1987

The year began with many pundits predicting a general election before the year was over, though none of the parties were in a particularly advantageous position. On the other hand, almost two in three of the public favoured the Conservatives to win the next election. The government was well into its privatisation policy, with British Telecom, the TSB, British Gas and British Airways successfully launched. The share-owning democracy, however, had not come about, with only one in five of the public owning shares, one-half of whom were Conservative supporters. When asked to look forward to the state of things after the next election if the Conservatives won, majorities predicted more encouragement for small businesses, more spent on defence, more unemployment, but less trade union power. When a similar question was asked in mid-February about the possible consequences of a Labour victory, majorities foresaw more union power, more direct taxation, more inflation, but less spent on defence. People were also asked in mid-February which of 12 items should be discussed at the next election. The top three items were unemployment (77 per cent), the National Health Service (60 per cent) and education (54 per cent). In 1983, the top three items had been unemployment (89 per cent), the cost of living (54 per cent) and the National Health Service (46 per cent).

To test the potential for tactical voting at the next election, Gallup asked a number of questions in mid-March on peoples' perceptions of the political pecking order in their area. Naturally, given Mrs Thatcher's majority in the 1983 election, the Conservatives had a 9-points lead as the party people expected to win in their area. Two in five, twice as many as for either of the other main parties, thought that the Alliance would be in second place. When asked who they would not like to win in their area, around one in three mentioned the Conservatives, one in three Labour and just one in 25 the Alliance. People were then asked what they would do in the classical tactical voting situation - their party was going to do badly; the party they disliked most was going to win; but the party in second place stood a chance of winning. A little over one in four said that in such a situation they would consider voting for the party in second place. The problem in March, however, was that only one in ten of the public actually perceived their area as fitting the classical pattern and even fewer - 3 per cent in all - were inclined to vote tactically.

Throughout the nation as a whole, following by-elections in Greenwich and Truro, and the Budget, the Alliance moved into second place, 6 points behind the Conservatives. Overall, the public reacted favourably to the Budget, though there were some doubts on its impact in some important areas. One in two thought that it was a fair one and one in two felt that Mr Lawson was doing a good job as Chancellor of the Exchequer. On the other hand, the public felt that, if anything, the Budget was not tough enough and did little to make them favourably inclined towards the government. Majorities also felt that it would not help the unemployed young, would not reduce unemployment, would not create more jobs, would not encourage people to work harder and would not make it easier for people in general to manage. Labour was still in third place in April, 12.5 points behind the Conservatives, but, perhaps of more importance, Mr Kinnock's personal rating had slipped to its lowest since he became party leader, with only one in four thinking he was a good leader. Two in three of the public agreed with the statement 'Labour party leadership is poor now' and similar proportions felt that Labour had become too extreme and was still suffering from its long-term image problem - disunity.

The local council elections, however, did not bring the sweeping gains the Alliance was hoping for to keep their momentum going and their standing in the polls fell as the country found itself in yet another general election campaign. The election turned out to be very similar to 1983: the Conservatives had a comfortable advantage over the other two parties, one which they never really looked like losing. The main difference between 1983 and 1987 was that Labour was being led by Neil Kinnock rather than Michael Foot and were more secure than 4 years earlier. The Alliance's expected, hoped for, surge in support never came and the mould of British politics remained very much in one piece.

The Alliance, following their disappointing result, literally fell apart as internecine divisions appeared between the two parties and within the individual parties themselves. Neither were to be healed by the end of the year. The ratings of both party leaders fell between June and July, from 51 per cent to 42 per cent for Mr Steel and from 48 per cent to 40 per cent for Dr Owen, who subsequently resigned as party leader, his position being taken by Robert Maclennan. Asked in July how they would vote in a by-election where there were 4 candidates - one each from the two main parties, a Liberal and one from an independent SDP led by Dr Owen - 12 per cent said that they would support the Liberal and 9 per cent opted for the SDP candidate. The image of a united Alliance, held by a majority (53 per cent) in May, fell badly soon after the election, so that in mid-June only 9 per cent thought that the two parties were united, while 79 per cent saw them as divided.

In contrast to the 1983 election, where a majority had thought that Mr Steel had performed well for his party on television, his critics outnumbered his supporters by two to one in the 1987 election. Dr Owen's television performances, too, were thought on balance not to have increased support for the Social Democrats. His subsequent resignation was seen as a bad thing for his party, though the public were more evenly divided on whether it would be good or bad for the Alliance. The public's initial rating of Mr Maclennan reflected very much his unknown qualities, three in four not being able to say whether he was proving a good leader or not. The proportion still stood at six in ten at the end of the year, but more worrying for the SDP was the fact that the decline in the undecideds had just gone to swell the growing number of Mr Maclennan's detractors.

Three items dominated the political scene in the second half of the year: the government's proposals for a community charge, their proposals on the reform of education and the state of the National Health Service. The first of these, the so-called 'poll tax', can be briefly stated: the more the public became aware of the proposition, the more unpopular it became and it was thought to be less fair than the unfair system it was supposed to be replacing. Between February 1986 and July 1987, for example, the balance of opinion went from a net positive position to a two to one negative position, and the proportion thinking it was fairer than the present rates system fell from 50 per cent to 27 per cent, with a considerable increase in those who thought it was not fair. When asked to choose between a number of possible options, a local income tax was the most popular, chosen by almost four in ten adults, followed by the current rates system, with a community charge chosen by around one in six.

Education is one of those issues which bubbles along in the public's consciousness, hardly ever being seen as the 'most urgent problem', but consistently being mentioned as one of the top half-dozen problems, particularly in terms of falling standards. In September Gallup conducted a major study among parents of children at state schools to measure their attitudes towards proposed changes in the education system. On balance, for example, parents felt that the general standard of education at their child's school had fallen, though around four in five were satisfied with the education that they were getting. One in two (54 per cent) felt that they actually had a choice as to which school their children went to, but almost as many (42 per cent) thought that it was really decided by the local educational authorities, and only 14 per cent said that they would apply for a transfer if another local school had places available. Seven in ten parents supported the idea of national written tests at the ages of 7, 11 and 14, and two in three supported the idea of a national core curriculum. On the other hand, only one in five were in favour of their child's school 'opting out' of local education authority control to become self-managing by boards of governors and the same low proportion thought that it was necessary for parents to get involved in the hiring and firing of head teachers or staff. The prospects for racial harmony were not particularly good, as measured by the replies to some of the questions. Fewer than one in two parents (45 per cent) said that they would agree to send their children to a school where more than half the children were from a different ethnic background to their own, and nine in ten of the remainder would disagree to do so even in the interests of racial integration.

In July, September and in December, people were asked which two issues were most important in helping them to decide how to vote. A similar question had also been asked during the election campaign. During the election and in the three post-election studies, the Health Service and jobs were the top two issues chosen, normally with around one in three choosing them, but this dramatically changed in December. Then, one in two mentioned the Health Service and almost as many gave it as one of the top two urgent problems facing the country, second only to unemployment. Paradoxically, both were 'good' issues for Labour but the Conservatives ended the year 12 points ahead of them. This was also in spite of nine in ten disapproving of proposals to scrap free dental checks and free eye tests.

On 19 October, 'Black Monday', share prices fell sharply around the world, reminding people of what had happened 60 years before and that the value of shares did not always move in an upward direction. Two in three of the public, however, felt that they would not be affected by the fall and almost as many thought that the economic situation was better than it had been in the 1930s. Furthermore, a little over one in two felt that the situation in the stock market would improve fairly soon, though one in three took the pessimistic view that it would be a long-term problem. One in three also thought that it would lead to an economic recession around the world, but only one in five felt that it would lead to one in Britain.

At the end of the year, Mrs Thatcher was voted the most admired woman, followed by other perennial favourites, Mother Teresa, the Queen and Princess Anne. Mr Gorbachev topped the list of admired men, closely followed by Bob Geldof, Terry Waite, Prince Charles and the Pope. Surprisingly perhaps, Mr Reagan did not figure in the upper echelons of acclaim. Snooker champion Steve Davis and racing driver Nigel Mansell shared first place as sports personality of the year, with Fatima Whitbread, the world's women's javelin champion, in third place. The BBC topped the list of best television programmes of the year, with 'Eastenders' and 'Bread', with Channel Four's 'Brookside' in third place, followed by 'The Bill' and 'The Charmer', both from ITV. 'Crocodile Dundee' was voted best film of the year and no other film obtained enough votes to make its inclusion on the list worthwhile.

Finally, Gallup asked one of its longest-running set of questions - the end-of-year poll, started in 1957. This asks people, normally in December, to look forward to the coming year and to say what they think will happen in general, and specifically to prices, employment, industrial relations, taxation, the economy and to international relations. On balance, 1988 was looked forward to as being better than 1987, though by a smaller margin than people had viewed 1987 in late 1986. However, the net figure was positive for the sixth year in succession, something which had not occurred since the early 1960s. Obviously the new year was thought to be one of rising prices, two in three thought so, but this was distinctly lower than the nine in ten, and higher, found in the late 1960s and early 1970s. Similarly, although 1988 was thought to be a year of rising unemployment, the one in three thinking so was the lowest since 1965, when one in two actually thought that there would be full employment. The 1987 view of relative industrial peace in 1988, for the third successive year, ended 30 years of gloomy forecasts on the industrial front. Possibly because total taxation had risen under Mrs Thatcher, despite promises to the contrary, the public continually looked forward to the coming year with anticipations of falling taxes and the 37 per cent who did so in 1987 were no exception. Only twice, in 1959 and in 1977, had the figure been beaten, but in four of the years since the Conservatives had regained power in 1979, more than 30 per cent forecast a drop in taxes. Naturally, the public's views on the economy had improved over earlier years, though they were still gloomy. The 22 per cent expecting economic prosperity had only been exceeded twice in the last two decades and only four times in the 1960s.

This sense of well-being on the domestic front extended to the wider sphere, with 26 per cent, the highest proportion since 1977, thinking that the coming year would be peaceful, more or less free of international disputes. Two in five, though, feared a troubled year with much international discord. The final three questions in the series dealt with the public's perception of the power of the three super powers, Russia, the United States and China. As far as attitudes to Russian power were concerned, there had been significant changes over the 30 or so years of the series. In the late 1950s and throughout the 1960s and 1970s, for example, around one in four more on average saw Russia's power increasing rather than decreasing. This average rose to more than one in three towards the early 1980s, then slumped, so that at the end of 1987 there were more Britons thinking that Russia's power would decline than saw it increasing. A similar pattern, though with some differences, occurred in the perceptions of America's power. The series started at a relatively low point with a net index of +3 (increasing power minus decreasing power). It rose steadily to peak at +33 in 1964, but fell back to the then all-time low of -10 in 1973. The trend was reversed and a decade later the all-time high of +44 was achieved. The 'down-wave', however, was at a faster rate than previously and the 1987 net index was -18, the worst ever for the United States. China was added to the series in 1965 and for the whole of the period upto and including 1987, more people have predicted an increase in Chinese power than have predicted a downturn. In the early 1970s, the figure was as high as +61 but fell to around half that amount during the 1980s.

Appendix: Tables

Year	General Elections	Conser-vative	Labour	Liberal	Others	Mean Error(1)
1945	Actual	39.3	48.0	9.2	2.7	
	Gallup (2)	+ 1.7	- 1.8	+ 1.3	- 1.2	1.5
1950	Actual	43.0	46.8	9.3	0.9	
	Gallup	+ 0.5	- 1.8	+ 1.2	+ 0.1	0.9
1951	Actual	47.8	49.3	2.6	0.3	
	Gallup	+ 1.7	- 2.3	+ 0.4	+ 0.2	1.2
1955	Actual	49.3	47.3	2.8	0.6	
	Gallup	+ 1.7	+ 0.2	- 1.3	- 0.6	1.0
1959	Actual	48.8	44.6	6.0	0.6	
	Gallup	+ 0.7	+ 0.4	- 0.5	- 0.6	0.6
1964	Actual	42.9	44.8	11.4	0.9	
	Gallup	+ 1.6	+ 1.7	- 2.9	- 0.4	1.9
1966	Actual	41.5	48.8	8.6	1.1	
	Gallup	- 1.5	+ 2.2	- 0.6	- 0.1	1.1
1970	Actual	46.2	43.8	7.6	2.4	
	Gallup	- 4.2	+ 5.2	- 0.1	- 0.9	2.8
1974	Actual	38.1	37.2	19.3	5.4	
(Feb)	Gallup	+ 1.4	+ 0.3	+ 1.2	- 2.9	1.5
1974	Actual	36.6	40.2	18.8	4.4	
(Oct)	Gallup	- 0.6	+ 1.3	+ 0.2	- 0.9	0.8
1979	Actual	45.0	37.8	14.2	3.0	
	Gallup	- 2.0	+ 3.2	- 0.7	- 0.5	1.6
1983	Actual	43.5	28.3	26.0	2.2	
	Gallup	+ 2.0	-1.8	0	- 0.2	1.0
1987	Actual	43.3	31.5	23.1	2.1	
	Gallup	- 2.3	+ 2.5	+ 0.4	- 0.6	1.5

Election for European Parliament

1979	Actual	50.6	33.0	13.1	3.3	
	Gallup	+ 0.4	+ 5.0	- 3.6	- 1.8	2.7

EEC Referendum

1975	Actual	Turnout: 64.5	'Yes' 67.5		
	Gallup	+ 0.5	+ 0.5		0.5

Notes: 1. The mean error is the average of the deviations of the final Gallup Poll from the actual result for each party (Great Britain only).

2. Gallup final poll figures are given as deviation from the election results for each party

154

Table 2 : Prime Ministers' Popularity : 1945-1987

Q. Are you satisfied or dissatisfied with ... as Prime Minister?

Government:		High	Low	Average
1945-51	Labour			
	Attlee (Aug 1945-Sept 1951)	66	37	47
1951-55	Conservative			
	Churchill (Dec 1951-Jan 1955)	56	48	52
	Eden (April/May 1955)	73	71	72
1955-59	Conservative			
	Eden (July 1955-Dec 1956)	70	41	55
	Macmillan (Feb 1957-Aug 1959)	67	30	50
1959-64	Conservative			
	Macmillan (Feb 1960-Oct 1963)	79	35	52
	Home (Nov 1963-Sept 1964)	48	42	45
1964-66	Labour			
	Wilson (Nov 1964-Feb 1966)	66	48	59
1966-70	Labour			
	Wilson (Apr 1966-June 1970)	69	27	41
1970-74	Conservative			
	Heath (Sept 1970-Feb 1974)	45	31	37
1974-79	Labour			
	Wilson (Apr 1974-Mar 1976)	53	40	46
	Callaghan (Apr 1976-Apr 1979)	59	33	46
1979-83	Conservative			
	Thatcher (June 1979-June 1983)	52	25	39
1983-87	Conservative			
	Thatcher (July 1983-June 1987)	53	28	39

Table 3 : Opposition Leaders' Popularity : 1955 - 1987

Q. Do you think ... is or is not proving a good leader of the ... party?

Government:	High	Low	Average
1955-59 Conservative			
Gaitskell (May 1956-Aug 1959)	53	32	43
1959-64 Conservative			
Gaitskell (Feb 1960-Jan 1963)	57	35	47
Wilson (Mar 1963-Sept 1964)	67	44	59
1964-66 Labour			
Home (Nov 1964-July 1965)	41	32	37
Heath (Aug 1965-Feb 1966)	51	40	47
1966-70 Labour			
Heath (Apr 1966-June 1970)	46	24	33
1970-74 Conservative			
Wilson (Sept 1970-Feb 1974)	66	37	49
1974-79 Labour			
Heath (Apr 1974-Jan 1975)	38	29	33
Thatcher (Feb 1975-Apr 1979)	64	31	41
1979-83 Conservative			
Callaghan (June 1979-Oct 1980)	63	46	53
Foot (Nov 1980-June 1983)	38	14	21
1983-87 Conservative			
Foot (July 1983-Sept 1983)	11	9	10
Kinnock (Oct 1983-June 1987)	58	26	40

Table 4 : Ratings of the War-time Prime Ministers

Q. In general, do you approve or disapprove of Mr... as Prime Minister?

Chamberlain		Approve	Disapprove	Churchill		Approve	Disapprove
1938	Oct	51	39	1942	Jan	89	7
	Nov	49	40		Feb	82	11
	Dec	51	40		Mar	81	13
1939	Jan	53	41		Apr	82	13
	Feb	56	35		May	87	8
	Mar	52	38		Jun	86	9
	Apr	55	38		Jul	78	15
	May	53	43		Aug	82	11
	Jun	53	42		Sept	82	10
	Aug	55	38		Oct	83	11
	Oct	65	29		Nov	91	7
	Nov	68	27		Dec	93	5
	Dec	64	30	1943	Jan	91	7
1940	Jan	56	32		Mar	90	7
	Feb	59	30		Jun	93	4
	Mar	57	36		Aug	93	5
	May	32	58		Nov	91	6
				1944	Jan	89	7
					Mar	86	10
Churchill					Apr	88	9
					Jun	91	7
1940	Jul	88	7		Aug	89	8
	Oct	89	6		Sept	89	8
	Nov	88	7		Oct	91	7
1941	Jan	85	7	1945	Jan	81	16
	Mar	88	7		Feb	85	11
	Jun	87	9		Mar	87	10
	Oct	84	11		Apr	91	7
	Dec	88	8		May	83	14

Table 5 : Satisfaction with Government's Conduct of the War

Q. In general, are you satisfied or dissatisfied with the Government's conduct of the war?

		Satisfied	Dissatisfied
1939	Nov	61	18
1940	Feb	59	19
1941	Jun	58	30
	Aug	61	25
	Oct	44	38
1942	Mar	35	50
	Apr	50	38
	May	63	24
	Jun	57	26
	Jul	42	41
	Aug	45	38
	Sept	41	37
	Oct	49	35
	Nov	75	17
	Dec	75	19
1943	Jan	72	20
	Mar	76	15
	Jun	75	13
	Aug	81	12
	Nov	74	17
1944	Jan	69	16
	Mar	70	19
	Apr	75	16
	Jun	80	13
	Aug	79	13
	Sept	86	8
	Oct	81	12
1945	Jan	72	20
	Feb	77	14
	Mar	83	12
	Apr	86	9
	May	87	10

158

Table 6 : Ideal Family Income and Amount Spent on Food : 1937-1987

Q. How much income per week do you think a family of four, including husband, wife and two children needs for health and comfort? (Average to nearest pound)

Q. About how much a week would you say you spend on food for your family, including milk? (Average to nearest pound)

	Ideal income	Expenditure on food
1937	6	na
1949	8	3
1950	9	4
1951	9	na
1952	10	4
1953	10	na
1957	na	5
1958	na	5
1959	na	6
1961	16	na
1964	18	na
1965	17	6
1966	20	9
1967	21	7
1968	22	7
1970	25	8
1972	31	10
1973	33	11
1974	41	12
1975	50	15
1976	56	18
1977	62	18
1978	74	22
1979	90	25
1982	141	30
1984	140	35
1986	154	37
1987	180	41

Table 7 : Rating of the Chancellor of the Exchequer and the Budget: 1949-1987

Q. Do you think that .... is doing a good job or a bad job as Chancellor of the Exchequer?
Q. Do you think the Budget is a fair one or not?

| | | Chancellor of the Exchequer | | | | Budget | |
		Good job	Bad job	Don't know	Fair	Not fair	Don't know
Cripps	Apr 1949	57	24	19		NA	
Butler	Apr 1952	49	25	26	60	32	8
	Apr 1953	63	31	6	50	37	13
	Apr 1954	53	31	16		NA	
	Apr 1955	57	18	25	50	32	18
Macmillan	Apr 1956	42	33	25	43	43	14
Thorneycroft	Apr 1957	50	23	27	42	40	18
Heathcoat	Apr 1958		NA		62	23	15
Amory	Apr 1959	58	18	24	56	34	10
	Apr 1960	43	28	29	41	47	12
Selwyn Lloyd	Apr 1961	36	31	33	33	51	16
	Apr 1962	42	30	28	48	34	18
Maudling	Apr 1963	59	19	22	59	24	17
	Apr 1964	47	33	20	41	48	11
Callaghan	Nov 1964	48	24	28	56	33	11
	Apr 1965	48	24	28	51	34	15
	May 1966	61	18	21	60	24	16
	Apr 1967	51	26	23	56	23	21
Jenkins	Apr 1968	41	28	31	43	47	10
	Apr 1969	49	32	19	59	32	9
	Apr 1970	61	19	20	66	24	10
Barber	Mar 1971	56	18	26	61	29	10
	Apr 1972	57	17	26	64	27	9
	Mar 1973	57	23	20	55	34	11
Healey	Mar 1974	43	22	35	56	32	12
	Nov 1974	53	23	24	59	27	14
	Apr 1975	44	36	20	51	37	12
	Apr 1976	60	23	17	63	23	14
	Apr 1977	38	46	16	36	54	10
	Nov 1977	58	23	19		NA	
	Apr 1978	57	27	16	68	24	8
Howe	Jun 1979	38	30	32	44	49	7
	Mar 1980	51	29	19	57	36	7
	Mar 1981	24	61	15	22	73	5
	Mar 1982	49	39	13	56	38	6
	Mar 1983	51	36	13	53	39	8
Lawson	Mar 1984	57	26	17	60	36	4
	Mar 1985	33	51	16	41	51	8
	Mar 1986	43	42	15	49	44	7
	Mar 1987	49	37	14	50	44	6

Table 8 : Standing of Trade Unions : 1952-1987

Q. Generally speaking, and thinking of Britain as a whole, do you think that trade unions are a good thing or a bad thing?

	Good thing	Bad thing	Don't know
1952	69	12	19
1954	71	12	17
1955	67	18	15
1956	61	20	19
1957	53	21	26
1958	61	15	24
1959	60	23	17
1960	59	16	25
1961	57	27	16
1963	62	21	17
1964	70	12	18
1965	57	25	18
1966	63	20	17
1967	60	23	17
1968	66	18	16
1969	57	26	17
1970	60	24	17
1971	62	21	17
1972	55	30	16
1973	61	25	14
1974	54	27	19
1975	51	34	16
1976	60	25	14
1977	53	33	14
1978	57	31	12
1979	51	36	13
1980	60	29	11
1981	56	28	16
1982	59	30	11
1983	63	25	12
1984	61	30	10
1985	65	24	10
1986	67	22	12
1987	71	17	12

Table 9 : End-of-Year Poll : 1957-1987

Q1 So far as you are concerned, do you think that 19.. (next year) will be better or worse than 19.. (this year)?

Q2 Which of these do you think is likely to be true of 19.. (next year)?

	Q1			Q2		
	Better	Worse	Same, don't know	Rising prices	Falling prices	Same, don't know
1957	39	6	55	52	21	27
1958	35	7	58	40	30	30
1959	46	6	48	39	32	29
1960	40	14	46	68	18	14
1961	38	18	44	75	7	18
1962	34	30	36	59	13	28
1963	54	7	39	70	11	19
1964	39	24	37	81	4	15
1965	42	21	37	79	7	14
1966	27	38	35	78	7	15
1967	22	48	30	89	3	8
1968	22	41	37	86	3	11
1969	40	17	43	84	5	11
1970	27	42	31	88	4	7
1971	42	28	30	85	4	11
1972	39	31	30	80	8	12
1973	25	46	29	88	6	6
1974	14	64	22	95	1	4
1975	31	35	33	78	6	16
1976	21	48	32	90	4	6
1977	53	18	29	56	15	29
1978	28	36	36	78	3	19
1979	16	66	18	89	2	9
1980	20	58	22	60	12	28
1981	30	40	30	76	4	20
1982	39	28	33	51	13	36
1983	36	34	29	69	5	25
1984	37	33	30	70	5	25
1985	37	28	36	59	7	35
1986	46	13	41	60	4	36
1987	38	31	30	65	4	30

The year indicated relates to the year in which the questions were asked. The results therefore relate to prospects in the following year.

Table 9 : End-of-Year Poll : 1957-1987 (contd)

Q3 Which of these do you think is likely to be true of 19.. (next year)?
Q4 Which of these do you think is likely to be true of 19.. (next year)?

	Q3			Q4		
	Full-employment	Rising unemploy-ment	Same, don't know	Strikes and industrial disputes	Industrial peace	Same, don't know
1957	34	37	29	48	18	34
1958	15	61	24	38	18	44
1959	38	36	26	46	16	38
1960	21	61	18	52	16	32
1961	29	41	30	45	14	41
1962	11	66	23	31	27	42
1963	48	22	30	40	17	43
1964	49	22	29	34	29	37
1965	49	29	22	55	21	24
1966	12	69	19	53	24	23
1967	19	58	23	60	14	26
1968	13	62	25	69	10	21
1969	26	42	32	64	15	21
1970	11	61	28	70	9	20
1971	11	63	27	56	16	28
1972	22	49	29	64	19	17
1973	39	35	26	77	10	13
1974	7	80	14	80	10	11
1975	9	74	16	53	29	18
1976	8	69	23	47	29	24
1977	15	38	47	65	9	26
1978	8	51	40	65	8	27
1979	6	72	22	72	6	21
1980	3	77	20	47	19	34
1981	3	72	24	62	12	27
1982	5	62	33	37	25	38
1983	6	52	43	55	16	29
1984	4	60	37	48	20	32
1985	4	51	45	31	30	39
1986	6	53	41	25	30	46
1987	12	33	54	29	31	40

The year indicated relates to the year in which the questions were asked. The results therefore relate to prospects in the following year.

Table 9 : End-of-Year Poll : 1957-1987 (contd)

Q5 Which of these do you think is likely to be true of 19.. (next year)?
Q6 Which of these do you think is likely to be true of 19.. (next year)?

	Q5			Q6		
	Taxes will rise	Taxes will fall	Same, don't know	Economic prosperity	Economic difficulty	Same, don't know
1957	38	18	44		NA	
1958	25	39	36		NA	
1959	23	41	36		NA	
1960	55	16	29	23	51	26
1961	56	9	35	15	51	34
1962	33	30	37	18	43	39
1963	48	22	30	43	20	37
1964	75	5	20	21	51	28
1965	68	9	23	32	40	28
1966	60	9	31	15	65	20
1967	82	5	13	13	63	24
1968	73	6	21	11	71	18
1969	57	17	26	32	39	29
1970	40	26	34	15	60	25
1971	35	33	32	19	52	28
1972	57	20	23	25	54	21
1973	66	7	27	14	67	19
1974	78	4	18	5	85	10
1975	65	8	27	12	73	16
1976	74	8	18	8	77	15
1977	19	43	38	26	36	39
1978	46	14	40	10	52	38
1979	40	8	52	6	77	17
1980	67	5	27	5	74	22
1981	68	12	20	4	72	24
1982	28	36	36	11	55	34
1983	65	7	28	13	53	33
1984	35	31	34	14	53	34
1985	26	25	49	10	45	45
1986	31	32	38	12	41	47
1987	31	37	33	22	36	42

The year indicated relates to the year in which the questions were asked. The results therefore relate to prospects in the following year.

Table 9 : End-of-Year Poll : 1957-1987 (contd)

Q7 Which of these do you think is likely to be true of 19.. (next year)?

Q8 Which of these do you think is likely to be true of 19.. (next year)?

	Q7			Q8		
	Peaceful, more or less free of inter- national disputes	Troubled with much inter- national discord	Same, don't know	Russia will in- crease her power in the world	Russian power will decline	Same, don't know
1957	31	33	36	48	18	34
1958	28	38	34	38	18	44
1959	52	21	27	46	16	38
1960	36	38	26	52	16	32
1961	13	56	31	45	14	41
1962	31	34	35	31	27	42
1963	47	20	33	40	17	43
1964	32	33	35	37	13	50
1965	18	59	23	40	20	40
1966	26	46	28	42	15	43
1967	24	43	33	48	12	40
1968	24	47	29	51	11	38
1969	34	39	27	43	15	42
1970	23	45	32	42	9	49
1971	16	61	23	39	13	48
1972	25	55	20	29	21	51
1973	20	61	18	35	13	52
1974	14	69	17	43	9	49
1975	26	53	21	44	12	44
1976	24	47	29	44	10	47
1977	33	33	34	39	9	53
1978	16	45	39	48	8	43
1979	7	69	24	41	6	54
1980	10	64	26	50	6	43
1981	15	55	29	36	13	50
1982	21	43	36	43	9	49
1983	11	66	23	40	11	50
1984	23	42	35	24	14	63
1985	18	42	40	25	11	64
1986	16	44	41	23	12	65
1987	26	40	34	20	25	56

The year indicated relates to the year in which the questions were asked. The results therefore relate to prospects in the following year.

Table 9 : End-of-Year Poll : 1957-1987 (contd)

Q9 Which of these do you think is likely to be true of 19.. (next year)?

Q10 Which of these do you think is likely to be true of 19.. (next year)?

	Q9			Q10		
	America will increase her power in the world	American power will decline	Same, don't know	China will increase her power in the world	China's power will decline	Same don't know
1957	30	27	43		NA	
1958	34	18	48		NA	
1959	39	21	40		NA	
1960	46	21	33		NA	
1961	39	16	45		NA	
1962	45	15	40		NA	
1963	43	16	41		NA	
1964	43	10	47		NA	
1965	47	17	36	47	13	40
1966	42	19	39	54	10	36
1967	38	25	37	43	15	42
1968	44	19	37	42	11	47
1969	44	21	35	49	12	39
1970	32	22	46	52	6	41
1971	29	28	43	64	3	32
1972	38	23	39	57	6	37
1973	24	34	42	46	6	49
1974	27	29	44	42	6	52
1975	30	27	43	48	6	46
1976	40	17	43	41	9	49
1977	30	16	54	42	5	53
1978	31	23	46	52	5	43
1979	35	19	45	50	2	49
1980	45	11	45	39	4	57
1981	43	11	46	39	5	55
1982	43	15	42	42	4	55
1983	54	10	36	35	6	59
1984	42	11	47	38	6	56
1985	38	10	56	32	4	64
1986	31	16	54	35	4	60
1987	18	36	47	36	6	59

The year indicated relates to the year in which the questions were asked. The results therefore relate to prospects in the following year.

Index